His Many Mansions

His Many Mansions

A
COMPILATION
of
CHRISTIAN BELIEFS

Illustrated

WITH DIAGRAMS OF THE INTRICATE AND
INTERESTING ORGANIZATIONS OF THE
LEADING CHRISTIAN CHURCHES WHICH
HAVE HERE BEEN CONDENSED FOR THE
FIRST TIME INTO AN AUTHORITATIVE AND
UNDERSTANDABLE FORM.

By
RULON S. HOWELLS

NEW YORK
THE GREYSTONE PRESS
1940

COPYRIGHT 1940 BY RULON S. HOWELLS
PUBLISHED 1940

All rights reserved

PRINTED IN THE UNITED STATES OF AMERICA
THE WILLIAM BYRD PRESS, INC.
RICHMOND, VIRGINIA

CONTENTS

PAGE

COMPARATIVE CHART OF TEN LEADING
    CHURCHES ON TWENTY-THREE QUESTIONS *Insert*

PART I

I. INTRODUCTION 7
II. INTRODUCTORY NOTES ON CHURCH ORGANIZATION
    AND GOVERNMENT 15
III. FORMAL CHRISTIAN CREEDS AND DOCTRINES . 20

PART II

A BRIEF HISTORY, DOCTRINE AND CHURCH GOVERNMENT OF THE FOLLOWING DENOMINATIONS

IV. ADVENTISTS 33
    Diagram Chart 37
V. BAPTISTS 43
    Diagram Chart 56
VI. CHURCH OF CHRIST, SCIENTIST 62
    Diagram Chart 67
VII. CHURCH OF JESUS CHRIST OF LATTER-DAY SAINTS 69
    Diagram Chart 80
VIII. CONGREGATIONAL AND CHRISTIAN CHURCHES . . 94
    Diagram Chart 100

CONTENTS—*continued*

	PAGE
IX. DISCIPLES OF CHRIST	106
Diagram Chart	110
X. EASTERN ORTHODOX CHURCHES (Catholic)	114
Diagram Chart	122
XI. EPISCOPAL, CHURCH OF ENGLAND	130
Diagram Chart	142
XII. LUTHERANS	152
Diagram Chart	163
XIII. METHODISTS	170
Diagram Chart	178
XIV. PRESBYTERIANS	190
Diagram Chart	198
XV. ROMAN CATHOLIC CHURCH	203
Diagram Chart	211
XVI. UNITARIANS	229
Diagram Chart	235
ACKNOWLEDGMENT AND CONTRIBUTING AUTHORITIES OF EACH DENOMINATION	239
SPECIAL REFERENCES	246
APPENDIX	248
INDEX	251

His Many Mansions

Part I

COMPARATIVE CHART OF TEN CHRISTIAN DENOMINATIONS ON TWENTY-THREE DOCTRINAL QUESTIONS

(See insert—back cover)

EXPLANATION OF COMPARATIVE CHART

The comparative doctrinal chart of the various churches, which accompanies this book, inserted in the back cover, is designed to show in a brief way some of the similarities and differences in the doctrines of the leading Christian Churches.

The form in which this is presented is such as to give in perspective the whole matter at a glance, thus allowing a comparative study of the subjects with as little difficulty as possible.

The Churches here chosen for study represent the largest membership and the most diversified, as to doctrine, of all Christian denominations.

The particular subjects were chosen with the purpose of covering the doctrinal basis of general Christian belief. In obtaining this information, it has been the endeavor of the compiler to obtain only the generally accepted Church doctrine and not any individual or personal viewpoint.

It must be remembered, however, that the diversity to be found within a denomination itself is as striking as the diversity between the various denominations themselves.

CHAPTER I

INTRODUCTION

In all walks of life men and women consult each other, compare notes, adopt procedures and principles when any legitimate gain can be made regardless of the source. The only exception seems to be in the field of religion.

An extensive but unsuccessful search for an unbiased book or compilation on the subject handled within these covers, prompted the author to assemble the contents of this book and arrange it in such form that one need not be a student of religion to read and understand it.

The aim of this book is to let various authorities representing different denominations or religious movements have the opportunity of presenting their own side or interpretation of Christian principles, explaining their own theories or theologies and bringing them together side by side so anyone can with little study see their likenesses and differences, thus gaining a composite picture of Christian Religion.

Too much has already been written by writers telling and interpreting what others believe rather than letting each speak for himself.

Although the American churches may differ to some extent in their organizations and on some points of doctrine from their European relatives, yet in the main those of the same general denomination are practically alike.

It has been the constant aim of the compiler to assemble

the accepted doctrines of each church as a whole, and not the varying individual beliefs. If one compares the doctrine that the church, as a church, subscribes to, with what a great number of people within the church actually believe, the difference is astounding.

While in a general way the members of all denominations advance in study, thought and expression, the creedal doctrine which their church in particular subscribes to does not so advance or is not elastic enough to meet the changing needs. There seems to be a need of revision, particularly in the expression of doctrine, to meet the needs of a changed and still changing world. It is apparent that the churches are not keeping step with a large part of their membership when actual inventory of personal belief is taken.

A considerable number of ministers also bear out this thought when they say, "Personally, I believe such and such, but my church as a whole would not so subscribe."

Most people acquire their religion from their parents, either Methodists, Anglicans, Catholics or some other, and then remain as such defending their membership or nominal adherence passively or if occasion demands actively, more perhaps purely as a matter of family inheritance or tradition than from actual premeditated choice. "What was good enough for my parents is good enough for me."

Many people remain in their born religious status because theirs appears to them to be just as good as any other. Few even of the ardent church workers, aside from the ministry, delve very deeply into their church's doctrines, let alone investigating any other belief. By far the

INTRODUCTION

vast majority of active church members know or concern themselves little more than to be able to recite prayers or formulated rituals and creeds.

An investigative mind, however, will seek out the foundation doctrinal works, creeds, etc. upon or from which each church develops its theology, for the super-structure will usually be an elaboration or extension of its original doctrines facilitating an understanding of what any church professes to believe.

When one realizes that there are many thousands of books in print at the present time dealing exclusively with religious subjects, an idea of the enormous field to study is obvious. The reference works, books, etc., on church and denominational belief, theology and kindred subjects are very extensive. In fact, in most instances the writings themselves are too voluminous to attract any but the most thorough students of theology.

In the latest government census there are 213 denominations listed,* of which 155 are grouped in 23 "families." For example, under "Methodists" there are 19 separate and independent denominations, all holding to the general Methodist doctrinal principles, which as a group form one of the 23 so-called families.

Seventy-eight of the total number of listed churches in the census, baptize by immersion; 68 have optional forms of baptism (infants and adults, by sprinkling, pouring or immersion); 67 practice infant baptism. Thirty-nine of the total 213 churches do not require adherence to either creeds or confessions.

During the past ten years 19 churches have officially

*See list on page 248.

changed their names, and 14 separate and complete reorganizations have taken place. Ten newly organized churches have come into existence during the past 14 years and eight major church bodies have consolidated in the past 7 years.

In his book, "The Belief of 700 Ministers," Dr. George Herbert Betts of Northwestern University, calls attention to the changing trend of thought on basic theological questions. The book was published as a result of a questionnaire answered by 500 active ministers of the leading Protestant churches in and near Chicago, and 200 students studying for the ministry in five different theological schools in different parts of the country. Quoting from page 51, "On the question whether God is three distinct persons in one, 44 per cent of students as against 80 per cent of ministers-in-service accept this view; 21 per cent of students as against 7 per cent of ministers are uncertain; 35 per cent of students as against 13 per cent of ministers disbelieve the proposition, similarly for all other points of the list."

Dr. Betts emphasizes the fact that the percentages of variance in the affirmative and negative answers to his questionnaire, range from 5 to 98 per cent. It also shows that 80 per cent of the Lutheran ministry, as represented by 104 ministers, agree on one-half of the total questions asked, while the Methodists, as represented by 111 ministers, show 80 per cent agreeing on only one-fifth of the total questions. Other denominations range in their percentages between these two extremes.

Aside from the doctrinal viewpoint being at such a variance among the different churches; the methods of

INTRODUCTION

church governments and organizations are particularly noticeable. It will be observed that the church organizations of some denominations are very complicated, while others are comparatively simple.

In conjunction with this compilation, a large number of young people of the various denominations were interviewed as to their particular interest in their church. Invariably the answer was that the church and its activities in a strictly religious way is something that can be attended to later in life. Generally there appears to be a lack of "youth appeal" in the services and activities of the churches.

A true conception of the Christ-like religion and the living of it should not make a person conspicuously pious in the sense of a commonly called "goody-goody" person or the like. One of the greatest problems facing the ministry today is to create an incentive for the youth to become actively church-minded or religiously inclined in somewhat of a practical way.

Many thinking students of religion have expressed the thought that if ministers would return to the simple doctrines concerning Diety, religion would be much simpler and easier to understand. They point to the old-fashioned or anthropomorphic God which men, inspired by the divine spirit, taught the ancients in the beginning of our conscious existence. Also if a comprehensible understanding could be agreed upon that is within the grasp and reach of normal average people, of God as our real and tangible Heavenly Father in whose actual image and likeness man was created and not in just some spiritual and undefinable sense, such as one finds in the Nicene and

Athanasian Creeds, much could be accomplished. That this God is a personage and has an operating influence, not merely as some undetermined mysterious and unfathomable force, but as an individual entity who perhaps actually went through what we are now going through and experiencing. Many think that with such a belief we could realize that He could really understand us. Teachers of religion would then be giving a comprehensive model of a perfect being whose infinite and personal attributes all mankind could strive to emulate in some degree. As it is now so many ministers put forth a God whom they themselves admit they neither understand nor comprehend, and enshroud him with a cloud of mysticism, that a plain and rational thinking person is driven to the conclusion that perhaps it is easier to delegate religious theories and worries to the clergy.

It is interesting indeed to observe that there are over 200 different churches (U. S. census report) each claiming to be "Christ's" church, and that the Holy Bible is its catalogue and book of rules—the same source book for all and yet so many differences. Astonishing it is that so many systems and diametrically opposed theological theories can evolve out of the same set of rules.

One need only glance through the Apostles', Nicene and Athanasian Creeds to see what many Christian churches have been trying to persuade themselves to believe. Surely when the "source" of this book of rules is a Heavenly personage, then one would conclude that it was high time for some utterance from this "source" to come forth or make itself manifest in some direct way and untangle this confusion that everywhere exists among religious organizations. The Biblical record shows that God spoke directly to men in olden times. The Bible is filled with such occurrences but even before these Scriptures were given to the world, such things as God directly speaking to man apparently ceased to exist.

It should be of great concern to the thinking intellectual Christians that from various surveys, questionnaires and compiled statistics, it is estimated that eight out of ten church-going laymen, if asked whether their particular church believes so and so on a doctrinal point, cannot with any exactitude say yes or no; but can give only their personal belief or thought, which, peculiar but true, differs to quite an extent from the doctrinal creed which the church of their affiliation actually prescribes.

We study most things in life and ascertain their value by comparison. Are we Baptist, Catholic or Methodist, etc., because after a thorough study of their principles, we claim it as "the" way to worship God? Or are we members for other reasons, such as friendships, birth, family relationship or some other such reason?

Do we know, or concern ourselves over what our fellowmen believe when they "happen" to be affiliated with a church other than that in which we have membership? Could it be possible that their interpretation of religion could make us happier than ours has been able to do? Such thoughts are more current now than ever before.

Even a casual perusal of the contents of this book may make one realize that the great differences in doctrines of Christian Churches and their forms of organization must lead to the questions: "Can they all be of God?" "Could a Supreme Being be the author of such confusion in the interpretation of His mind and will?" On the other hand one might say that God allows His children to worship Him each in His own way though these ways be so widely different. Then again one would ask, "Do these diversified and too often contradictory 'ways' found among the churches lead to a truer love and understanding of one's fellowmen?" "Do the jealousies that exist among churches work for a 'unity' of faith and a better worship of God?"

One observing the confused panorama of Christian organizations might naturally ask himself "WHICH WAY—WHICH ONE?"

CHAPTER II

INTRODUCTORY NOTES ON CHURCH ORGANIZATION AND GOVERNMENT

To aid those interested in a fuller understanding of Christianity and of those organizations and systems which in the main constitute its organized framework, the church organization diagrams have been carefully and authoritatively prepared.

Much to the surprise of the author, no similar diagram plan of church organization has been heretofore worked out by any of the various denominations. Thus, considerable time was necessary in gaining the cooperation of the representative authorities of each of the denominations considered, to formulate in the manner and form here given, an accepted and approved interpretative graph of its organization.

A work that aims to give a brief and yet comprehensive view of the various organizations must on the one hand cultivate the art of brevity and on the other hand aim to be as complete as possible. It was this double duty that made the task difficult.

In the study of church government, it is well to keep in mind some of the general definitions and opinions prevalent as to what is meant by the word "church."

As understood today, there are at least two widely different opinions or classifications regarding the meaning of a church, both claiming the New Testament as authority. The first is, that Jesus Christ established a definite church with a code of laws pertaining to belief and government. The second is that he gave us only moral instruction and no definite laws of belief or discipline. Under the first classification may be grouped those who claim that Jesus Christ established only one church, and that the churches mentioned by Paul and others of the early missionaries, as recorded in the New Testament, were all parts of the one church. Still others hold that the Christian Churches of the New Testament were each separate and distinct in government, but one faith.

The Roman Catholic, Greek, Church of England and other Christian organizations with a generally recognized form of government, whether by presbyters or by the congregation, may be listed under the first above mentioned classification. Under the second will come all who hold that to observe the moral code as taught by Jesus Christ is all sufficient and a particular church affiliation is not necessary.

Forms of Church Government

Various bodies of Christians claim that many principles of their church government are derived or taken from the New Testament. Roman Catholics, Episcopalians, Presbyterians, Reformed Baptists and Congregationalists, whose governments are as different as possible, all believe that their respective systems of church government are derived from the Scriptures, particularly from the Gospels, the Acts of the Apostles and the Epistles.

INTRODUCTORY NOTES 17

Apostolic succession is of fundamental importance to the Roman Catholic, the Greek Catholic and the Anglican communion (Church of England). Each traces its succession of bishops, and hence of ordained ministers, back through the ages to one or another of the Apostles, and holds that since the time of Peter and Paul it has had an unbroken succession of the episcopal order. Churches using the presbyterian or congregational order hold that their respective systems are in harmony with the Scriptures and insist that they have a valid ministry. They do not accept the idea of apostolic succession, and do not believe that any particular system is of divine authority, but that Churches of Christ are free to adapt their form of government to circumstances and conditions, provided that the procedure be orderly.

To simplify church government (organization) for study, Christian Churches may be grouped into three distinct systems known as the congregational, the presbyterial and the episcopal. There are, however, many modifications or variations of these systems. It is not always possible to determine which one a particular denomination employs. For example the Lutherans in the United States generally classify themselves as congregational; some of them, however, contend that their system is presbyterial, while a few insist that it is really more nearly episcopal. In the Scandinavian countries the Lutheran is the state church and has bishops.

The first of the three distinct church governmental systems, as mentioned above, is the congregational method which recognizes the local church, or congregation, as having full control of its own affairs, and is not subject to legislative or executive direction by any denominational organization or even by the whole denomination itself. That is, each local church is a complete body in itself with inherent authority to determine its own doctrines and to conduct all the business appertaining to itself.

The second system is called "presbyterial" and is governed by presbyters, which is another word for elders. Presbyters are elder ministers, or teaching elders, bishops or pastors, and there are also in each local church, "ruling" elders, who are laymen, constituting with the pastor the session or consistory. Control in each church is exercised through the session or consistory. Then comes the presbytery composed of pastors and elders of the churches of a district; then the synod, consisting of representatives and presbyteries or classes, and then the General Synod or the General Assembly, the chief legislative and judicial authority of the denomination. All Presbyterian and Reformed Churches, including the Lutheran, generally use the presbyterial form of government, and, strictly speaking, that of the Methodists is more akin to the presbyterial than to the episcopal government, although they have bishops.

The third, or episcopal system, centers in the bishop. The Roman Catholic Church is governed by the pope as bishop of Rome, which it calls the primal Christian see. He creates cardinals, archbishops and bishops, calls ecumenical councils, at long intervals, to advise him, but he is always the supreme head of the church. The Anglican Communion (principally the Church of England) and the Eastern Orthodox Churches (Catholic) are also episcopally governed, though the state comes in to modify the system somewhat. The Protestant Episcopal Church of the United States has a triennial General Convention, composed of two houses, the house of bishops and the house of lay deputies. This is the supreme legislative body of that church.

The Methodist Episcopal Church, a type of a number of bodies similarly organized, lodges supreme legislative and judicial power in the General Conference, a body composed of ministerial and lay delegates.

A summary classification of church governments is as follows:

I. Episcopal form (those under authority of bishops), includes Roman Catholics, Eastern Orthodox (Catholics), most Methodists and Episcopalians and Moravians.

II. Synodical or Presbyterian form (those controlled by representative bodies), includes Presbyterians, Lutheran, Reformed and many Methodists, also many smaller denominations.

III. Congregational form (those who owe no authority above the individual church or congregation), includes Baptists, Congregationalists, Christians, Friends, Adventists, Unitarians, Universalists and Disciples of Christ.

IV. Distinct from the above classified forms are the Christian Scientists, Church of Jesus Christ of Latter-day Saints (Mormons) and some smaller denominations.

CHAPTER III

FORMAL CHRISTIAN CREEDS

A Summary of many basic doctrines of Faith which still form an important part of the theology of many leading churches

Following the apostacy and disorganization of the original Church, or organization established by Jesus Christ, and soon after the beginning of the Christian State Church (Rome and Constantinople) attempts were frequently made by both ecclesiastical and political authorities to have or formulate a crystallized summary of belief upon which general doctrinal issues and points could be agreed upon for the sake of clarity, uniformity and exposition among the various factions of the then Christian schools of thought.

Conventions and assemblies were called by political and ecclesiastical authorities wishing to have some sort of a summarized doctrine formed in an attempt to unify beliefs and to avoid the confusion and strife which periodically arose among ecclesiasts when a new wave of doctrine or interpretation swept over the then relatively small Christian world.

Schisms or splits occurred as religious leaders became aware of and converted to new ideas, interpretations and theories. One group opposed another until different factions, through political allies, threatened the Roman Empire whose leaders became more and more under the influence of the ecclesiastical heads.

Several momentous conclaves or assemblies were convened at which definite interpretations on doctrines were finally agreed upon, by free acceptance on the part of some and force or coercion on the part of others. There was never a complete unity of thought or accord at any assembly. The dominant Christian Church (Roman Catholic) through political power held matters more or less in control until the great wave of reformation came over Europe. (Beginning with Martin Luther reformers with the help of their sympathizers formed divergent groups, only however after first failing in their attempt to change the "Mother Church.") These new groups then set about to form their own creeds and doctrines. The basis, to a large extent, of the later creeds formed by the reforming groups was of course indirectly the Roman Catholic influence which the first reformers, up until the time they broke away, were generally under. Example—Martin Luther was formerly a Catholic priest; John Calvin a Chaplain also in the Roman Catholic Church.

The following are the most important creeds both Roman Catholic and Reformed, most of which are at present incorporated into or made a part of the fundamental doctrines of most present day Christian denominations:

The Apostles' Creed

"I believe in God, the Father Almighty, Creator of heaven and earth; and in Jesus Christ, His only Son, our Lord; who was conceived by the Holy Ghost, born of the virgin Mary, suffered under Pontius Pilate, was crucified, died and was buried. He descended into Hell; the third day He arose again from the dead; He ascended into Heaven, sitteth at the right hand of God, the Father Almighty; from thence He shall come to judge the living and the dead.

"I believe in the Holy Ghost, the holy Catholic Church, the communion of Saints, the forgiveness of sins, the resurrection of the body and life everlasting. Amen."

The Apostles' Creed is considered the earliest of the more important ecumenical creeds. It is not the production of the Apostles, nor does it belong to the apostolic age, but is a subsequent popular summary of the apostolic teaching.

It does not appear in its present form before 650 A.D. but its predecessors probably arose in Rome in the second or third century. It has two material differences from the Nicene Creed: (1) "He descended into hell (or darkness)," omitted in the Nicene; (2) "resurrection of the body;" in the Nicene, "of the dead." It is used by Roman Catholics privately and at baptism; it is much used by Protestants.

The Nicene Creed

"I believe in one God the Father Almighty; maker of heaven and earth, and of all things visible and invisible.

"And in one Lord Jesus Christ, the Only-Begotten Son of God, begotten of the Father before all the worlds (God of God), light of light, very God of very God, begotten, not made, being of one substance (essence) with the Father; by whom all things were made; who, for us men and for our salvation, came down from heaven, and was incarnate by the Holy Ghost of the virgin Mary, and was made man; and was crucified for us under Pontius Pilate; he suffered and was buried; and the third day he rose again, according to the scriptures; and ascended into heaven, and sitteth on the right hand of the Father; and he shall come again, with glory, to judge both the quick and the dead; whose kingdom shall have no end.

"And (I believe) in the Holy Ghost, the Lord and giver of life; who proceedeth from the Father (and the Son); who with the Father and the Son together is worshiped and glorified; who spake by the prophets. And (I believe) one Holy Catholic and Apostolic Church. I acknowledge one baptism for the remission of sins; and I look for the resurrection of the dead, and the life of the world to come. Amen."

It is usually described as a revision by the first Council of Constantinople, 381 A.D., of the creed adopted at Nicaea, 325 A.D.; although there are good grounds for the belief that it represents substantially a creed written or used by St. Cyril of Jerusalem. In the Western Church since the 11th century it has differed from the original in the significant words: "And in the Holy Ghost ... Who proceedeth from the Father and the Son" (qui ex Patre, Filioque procedit). The controversy between the Orthodox and Roman Catholic Churches on these words has made a shibboleth of the Filioque. The Nicene Creed is the official creed of Orthodox, Roman Catholic, Lutheran and some Protestant Churches.

THE ATHANASIAN CREED

"Whosoever will be saved: before all things it is necessary that he hold the Catholic faith: which faith except every one do keep whole and undefiled: without doubt he shall perish everlastingly.

"And the Catholic faith is this: that we worship one God in trinity, and trinity in unity; neither confounding the persons: nor dividing the substance (essence). For there is one person of the Father: another of the Son: and another of the Holy Ghost. But the Godhead of the Father, of the Son, and of the Holy Ghost, is all one: The glory equal, the majesty coeternal.

"Such as the Father is: such is the Son: and such is the Holy Ghost. The Father uncreate (uncreated): The Son uncreate (uncreated): and the Holy Ghost uncreate (uncreated). The Father incomprehensible (unlimited): The Son incomprehensible (unlimited): and the Holy Ghost incomprehensible (unlimited, or infinite).

"The Father eternal: the Son eternal: and the Holy Ghost eternal. And yet they are not three eternals: but one eternal. As also there are not three uncreated: nor three incomprehensibles (infinites): but one uncreated: and one incomprehensible (infinite). So likewise the Father is Almighty: the Son Almighty: and the Holy Ghost Almighty. And yet they are not three almighties: but One Almighty.

"So the Father is God: the Son is God: and the Holy Ghost is God. And yet they are not Three Gods: but One God. So likewise the Father is Lord: the Son Lord: and the Holy Ghost Lord. And yet not Three Lords: but One Lord. For like as we are compelled by the Christian verity: to acknowledge every person by himself to be God and Lord: so are we forbidden by the Catholic religion: to say, there be (are) Three Gods, or Three Lords.

"The Father is made of none: neither created, nor begotten. The Son is of the Father alone: not made, nor created: but begotten. The Holy Ghost is of the Father and of the Son: neither made, nor created, nor begotten: but proceeding. So there is One Father, not Three Fathers: One Son, not Three Sons: One Holy Ghost, not Three Holy Ghosts.

"And in this trinity none is afore, or after another: none is greater, or less than another (there is nothing before, or after: nothing greater or less). But the whole Three persons are coeternal, and coequal. So that in all things, as aforesaid:

the unity in trinity, and the trinity in unity, is to be worshiped. He therefore that will be saved, must (let him) thus think of the trinity.

"Furthermore it is necessary to everlasting salvation: that he also believe rightly (faithfully) the incarnation of our Lord Jesus Christ. For the right faith is, that we believe and confess: that our Lord Jesus Christ, the Son of God, is God and Man; God, of the substance (essence) of the Father; begotten before the worlds: and man, of the substance (essence) of his mother, born in the world. Perfect God: and perfect man, of a reasonable soul and human flesh subsisting.

"Equal to the Father, as touching his Godhead: and inferior to the Father as touching his manhood. Who although he be (is) God and man; yet he is not two, but one Christ. One; not by conversion of the Godhead into flesh: but by taking (assumption) of the manhood into God.

"One altogether; not by confusion of substance (essence): but by unity of person. For as the reasonable soul and flesh is one man: so God and man is one Christ; who suffered for our salvation: descended into hell (hades, spirit-world): rose again the third day from the dead.

"He ascended into heaven, he sitteth on the right hand of the Father God (God the Father) Almighty. From whence (thence) he shall come to judge the quick and the dead. At whose coming all men shall rise again with their bodies; and shall give account for their own works. And they that have done good shall go into life everlasting: and they that have done evil, into everlasting fire.

"This is the Catholic faith: which except a man believe faithfully (truly and firmly), he can not be saved."

The Athanasian Creed was completed in about the sixth century. Its origin is involved in obscurity, like that of the Apostles' Creed; but thought by most students to be of Latin origin. It furnishes one of the most remarkable examples of the extraordinary influence which works of unknown or doubtful authorship have exerted. The above printed Athanasian Creed is the old translation revised. It is held authoritative in the Roman Catholic, Lutheran and Anglican Churches.

NOTE: This creed is not called Athanasian because Athanasius was its author. It bears his name rather because it is supposed to embody the Catholic doctrines of the Trinity and the Incarnation, as understood by him.

Athanasius was born in Alexandria, Egypt, 293 A.D. and died 373 A.D. after an unusually stormy career.

In order to understand the purpose of the creed, some of the circumstances under which the doctrines it embodies took form, may be recalled.

When the emperor, Constantine, also called the Great, had gained recognition as the sole ruler of the empire, he found that there were a great many Christians in all parts of his wide domain. He shrewdly calculated that if he could win their support, he would be comparatively safe on the shaky throne; at least more so, than if he put his trust in the ruffians who constituted the main bulk of the army. Consequently, he began by abolishing edicts issued by former persecutors and promulgating laws favorable to the Christians.

But as he considered the expediency of the new policy, he discovered that the Christians were not united among themselves, but cut up into factions bitterly fighting and condemning each other. He comprehended that a body of Christians thus broken up would be useless as a political support. The Christians must be united and cease quarreling. In order to accomplish this, he ordered the Christian prelates to meet in a conference and get together on their doctrines. The meeting, or council was held under his auspices at Nicaea, 325 A.D.

FORMAL CHRISTIAN CREEDS

It was the Arian heresy that rent the church at the time.

The Arians taught that the Father is God; that he alone is "unbegotten," wise, good, unchangeable, and separated from man by an infinite chasm.

The Son of God, they held, is also pre-existent; he existed "before time and before the world," and "before all creatures." He is the perfect image of the Father, and the mediator between God and man. In a secondary sense, they admitted, he may be called "God," but he is, notwithstanding all this, created—the first of the creations of God, through whom he called other creatures into existence. He is, they maintained, "made" out of nothing. He is not eternal, because there was a time when he was not.

This was the main heresy with which Emperor Constantine's council had to deal.

Athanasius was in attendance at the council. He was then a young deacon in the church at Alexandria, but he was probably also the private secretary of Bishop Alexander of that city, and had, as such, access to the sessions of the council. Once there, he became, through his greater fund of information and superior oratory, the foremost among the opponents of Arius. It was, undoubtedly, he who gave form and substance to the Nicene creed.

When, later, it was found necessary, from the "orthodox" point of view, to amplify the doctrines incorporated in the Nicene creed, against Arian heretics, the "Athanasian Creed" was composed and published as containing the belief of Athanasius, in order to give it a prestige it could never have obtained on its own merits. It will be noticed that it is rather a polemical document than a creed.

THE AUGSBURG CONFESSION

Was first issued in 1530 and is the official statement of the Lutheran Churches. It was written by Melanchthon and endorsed by Luther. As it was prepared for the Diet of Augsburg, it does not include many condemnations of the Roman Catholic Church, but dwells principally on the positive beliefs of Luther.

The Thirty-nine Articles of the Church of England

The Thirty-nine Articles date in their present form from the beginning of Elizabeth's reign, when they were written by a group of bishops. They are Calvinistic in theological emphasis, and announce clearly the royal supremacy in the Church of England. They are official in the Church of England, and, with occasional changes in its various daughter churches (usually Episcopalian).

The Westminster Confession

Was issued 1645-47, and is the most celebrated pronouncement of English-speaking Calvanism. It is official in the Church of Scotland, with occasional changes in most of its daughter churches (usually Presbyterian), and among Congregationalists.

The Doctrine of Arminianism

This so-called Dutch theological doctrine is subscribed to as very important doctrine by many denominations of today. It received its name from the Dutch theologian Arminius 1560-1609.

It represented a reaction against certain principles of the Calvinistic doctrine and resisted the popular tendency of the day to erect everywhere a formulated creed.

Arminianism attempted to re-state what was regarded as the primitive and scriptural view held by the church before Augustine, concerning the relation between God and man in the work of salvation; maintaining that man was solely responsible for his own damnation, which was, of course, decidedly opposed to the Calvinistic doctrine of predestination.

The complete text of the Arminian articles of doctrine can be found in *Creeds of Christendom*, by Philip Schaff.

The Reformation

This term designates the ecclesiastical revolution which took place in the 16th century against certain doctrines and practices of the Roman Catholic Church.

Though primarily a religious revolution which attacked the universal supremacy of the pope and ended "religious unity" in Christendom, it was also accompanied by changes in the political, social and intellectual condition of western Europe.

Its leaders were called reformers; their purpose at first was to enact definite reforms within the Catholic Church. However, being persecuted for their attempts by the Catholic Church and making no headway in their original purpose, their followers branched out into the general Protestant Reformation, to which the Protestant Churches of today trace their beginning. The Reformers sought to justify their innovations by an appeal, from the Church's tradition, to the Scriptures.

In the 16th century A.D., generally known as the beginning of the Great Reformation, there was no effort in any part of Europe to develop broad tolerance; whatever religious group was in power forced, or tried to force, its views on the whole state by propaganda and the sword. The principal period of growth in the Reformation was its first 30 years (1520-50); by the middle of the century the Catholic Reform had got under way and was reclaiming the people to the Church in south and Rhenish Germany, in Austria, in Poland, and in Hungary, and was reaffirming its hold over them in the countries which had remained Catholic. A great advantage to the Roman Church lay in the divisions that rapidly developed among Protestants. The greatest of these lay in the split between Calvinism and Lutheranism. In his church in Geneva, John Calvin imposed the force of his personality to develop the most carefully built Protestant theology and the presbyterian form of church government. From Geneva, Calvinism spread to include the Protestantism of France (Huguenots), Scotland (Church of Scotland and Presbyterianism), the Netherlands and some parts of Germany (Reformed Churches). On the Continent Calvinists were distinguished from Lutherans by the term Reformed. Swiss Protestantism never lost the imprint of Zwingli, who believed in extending Protestantism by war and fell in battle at Cappel (1531) fighting Catholic Swiss. All over the continent another form of Protestantism, which was called Anabaptism, was powerful, especially among the lower classes. The Baptist organizations were formed from this movement. The Church of England went its own way, retaining its episcopacy, reforming its liturgy, and setting up the Calvinizing Thirty-nine Articles. The Reformation fundamentally altered the concepts of many peoples and deeply affected the economic and political history of Europe.

Part II

A Brief History, Doctrine and
Church Government of
Various Denominations

CHAPTER IV

ADVENTISTS

Those adhering to the Adventist doctrines are located principally in the United States of America. Missionary work of various kinds is carried on in practically every foreign country.

HISTORICAL SKETCH

Adventists compose a group of religious denominations whose distinctive doctrine centers in their belief concerning the second coming of Jesus Christ. The name Adventism is specifically applied to the teachings which grew out of the preaching of William Miller (a Baptist preacher) born 1782, who predicted the end of the world for 1843, then for 1844. When it did not occur, a meeting of the "Millerites," or Second Adventists, at Albany in 1845 adopted a statement declaring their belief that the visible return of Christ was to be expected, but at an indefinite time; that it would be the occasion of the resurrection of the dead, whether just or unjust; and that the millennium would then have its beginning. In 1845 the original body took the name of Evangelical Adventists. In 1866 the Church of God was formed as a result of division among the Seventh-day Adventists over the question of the prophecies of Mrs. Ellen Gould White. The observance of the seventh day is retained by the younger branch as one of their practices, which also include tithing. The Advent Christians date their beginning from the formation of a General Association in 1861. They believe that through faith in Christ all men may share salvation and enjoy immortality, but that for the wicked there is to be no future existence, since they are doomed to utter extinction. Similar views are held by the Life and Advent Union, organized in 1862, and the Age-to-Come Adventists (the Churches of God). The members of the latter branch look for an earthly kingdom under Christ upon His coming again. All believers are promised immortality and a share in the restoration of Israel, but for the wicked the end is destruction. In its beginning, the Adventist movement was wholly within the existing churches. In 1845, however, there was a general organization of the adherents of the Adventist doctrines.

Seventh-Day Adventists

History

A few persons in New England, formerly of the First-day Adventist, began in 1844 to observe the seventh day of the week, as Sabbath, and to preach the doctrines which now constitute the distinctive tenets of the Seventh-day Adventists. At a Conference, held in Battle Creek in 1860, these were organized under the name "Seventh-day Adventist Denomination," and three years later a General Conference was organized.

Doctrine

The Seventh-day Adventists have no formal or written creed, but take the Bible (the only infallible and authoritative rule of faith and life) as their rule of faith and practice, believing they were called of God to give the special message due this world and to carry out a program of world evangelization.

The following is a summary of the chief points of their belief:

The law of God is the divine standard of righteousness, binding upon all men. Christ, taking upon Himself the nature of the seed of Abraham, lived as an example, died as a sacrifice, was raised for justification, and is now the only mediator for man in the heavenly sanctuary, where, through the merits of "His shed blood," He ministers pardon and forgiveness of sins to all who come to God through Him.

The seventh day of the week, from sunset on Friday to sunset on Saturday, is the Sabbath established by God's law and should be observed as such. Immersion is the only proper form of baptism. Man is not by nature immortal, but receives eternal life only by faith in Christ. The state to which man is reduced at death is one of unconsciousness; that men at death go not to their reward or punishment immediately, but that they "sleep" until the day of the resurrection, the investigative judgment now in progress in heaven decides the eternal destiny of all men.

The personal, visible coming of Christ is near at hand and is to precede the millennium; at this coming the living righteous will be translated, and the righteous dead will arise and be taken to heaven, where they will remain until the end of the millennium. During the millennium the punishment of the wicked will be determined, and at its close Christ with His people will return to the earth, the resurrection of the wicked will occur, and Satan, the originator of all sin, will, together with his followers, meet final destruction.

The earth will be then made a fit abode of the people of God throughout the ages, where the righteous will dwell forever, and sin will never again mar the universe of God.

The Seventh-day Adventists make the use of intoxicants and tobacco in any form a ground for exclusion from church fellowship. They advocate the complete separation of church and state and oppose all religious legislation, by states.

They are strongly opposed to the so-called "higher criticism." The invitation to the sacrament of the Lord's Supper is general to all Christians, the decision as to participation resting with the individual.

The service of washing one another's feet, as recorded in John XIII, is observed at the quarterly meetings, the men and women meeting separately for this purpose, previous to the celebration of the Lord's Supper, during which they meet together.

With regard to the time of the Advent, they have never set a definite date, believing that it is near, but that the day and hour have not been revealed.

Organization and Government

The Seventh-day Adventists have a congregational form of government. Each local church is largely independent in its government, although under the general supervision of the conference of which it is a member.

ADVENTISTS

SEVENTH-DAY ADVENTISTS CHURCH
ORGANIZATION DIAGRAM

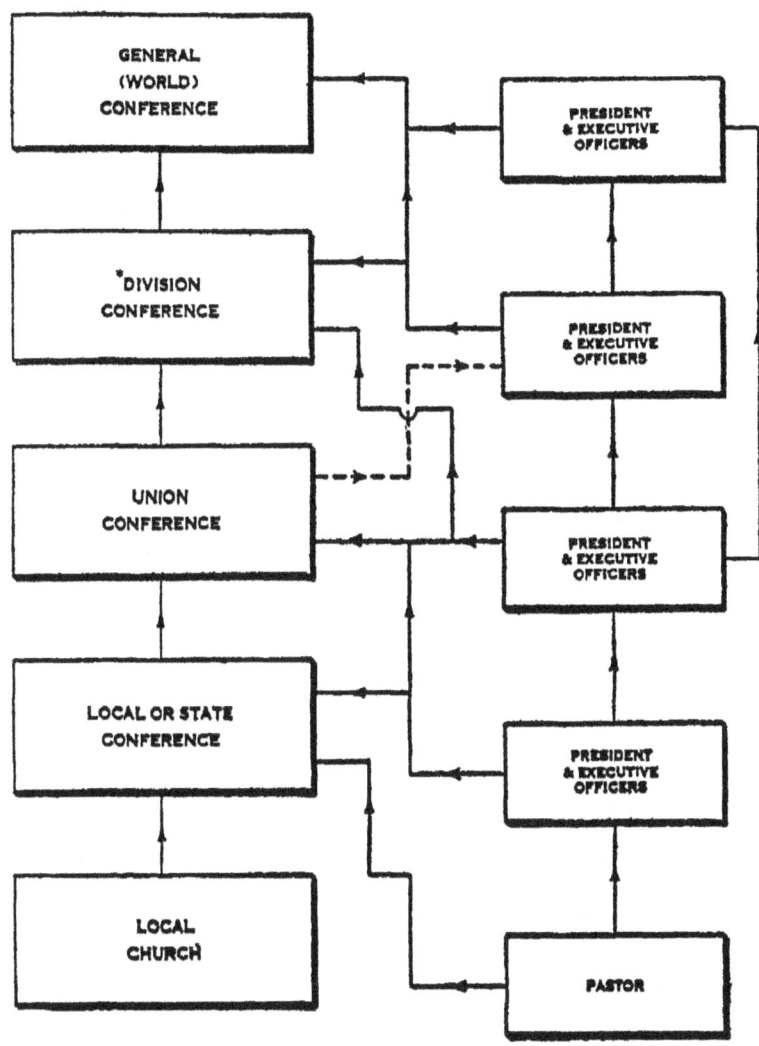

NOTE: ARROWS POINT TOWARD A HIGHER JURISDICTION OR PRESIDING OFFICIAL.
* IN NORTH AMERICA THE GENERAL CONFERENCE TAKES THE PLACE OF THE DIVISION CONFERENCE ALTHOUGH THERE IS A DIVISION PRESIDENT. THE DOTTED LINE APPLIES ONLY TO THE NORTH AMERICAN DIVISION.

Church organization is brought about by any ordained minister calling a meeting of the believers who desire to unite in church fellowship—after baptism the members proceed to elect officers; church elders, one or more; deacons, one or more; deaconesses, one or more; treasurer, clerk and missionary secretary. These officers are under the direction of the conference president with his executive committee. The conferences are usually made up by states. One or more elders are elected annually to care for the spiritual interests of the church, conduct services, and, in case of need, administer the sacraments. One or more deacons and deaconesses are also elected annually to care for the financial and administrative work. In the case of large congregations, particularly in cities, ordained ministers are sometimes appointed as pastors, but usually they act as itinerant evangelists, having supervision of a number of local churches, and directing their chief effort to missionary work in the development of new fields.

All the churches in a state form a state conference, to which they elect delegates, in the ratio of one to every fifteen members. The state conferences are united into groups of five or six, to form union conferences to which delegates are elected by the state conferences, on the basis of one for every two hundred church members. The union conferences throughout the world are united in the general conference composed of delegates from the union conferences in the ratio of one to every thousand church members.

The presidents of the local or state conferences and chairmen of state departments are ex officio members of the executive committees of their union conferences, and the presidents of the union conferences, together with the chairmen of union departments, constitute the executive committee of the General Conference. Membership in the conferences or the ministry is open to both sexes, although there are very few female ministers.

Applicants for church membership, not already members of a church, appear before the elders of the local church for examination. If approved, they are recommended for baptism at some public service, usually when the ordained minister in general charge can be present, though this is not essential. After baptism, either at the same or a subsequent service, they are presented to the church by the elders, and received by vote of the members present.

Applicants for ordination to the ministry are licensed to preach, for a limited term, by a conference, either state, union or general. At the expiration of that term, on approval by the conference, they are recommended for ordination, and are ordained, under supervision of the conference, by ministers selected for that service. This ordination is for life, but ministers are expected to renew their papers at each meeting of the conference which ordained them.

Local church expenses are met by special contributions, and collections are made during the year for the different departments of denominational work. The expenses of the ministry are met by the tithing system, each church member being expected to contribute a tenth of his income. The associations connected with state conferences usually hold in trust all the property for the local churches, while associations formed for union conferences hold property of a more general character.

The Local Church

Consists of the following:

> Pastor
> Board of Elders
> Board of Deacons
> Board of Deaconesses
> Treasurer
> Clerk
> Missionary Leader and Missionary Secretary
> Sabbath School Superintendent
> Young People's Leader

The above listed officials constitute the official board of the local church. The pastor acts as chairman of this board. In the absence of a pastor, a local elder may act as chairman of the Official Board. Other church members may be elected to the Official Board.

The local church does not engage the pastor, nor does it have power to dismiss him. The local church pays tithes to the local conference and is directly responsible in all matters to the local conference.

The Local or State Conference

It consists of an indefinite number of local churches, depending chiefly upon geographic conditions. It may be confined to boundaries of a state or there may be two or more local conferences within the same state. Every pastor is a delegate to the local conference and every

ADVENTISTS

local church is entitled to send delegates to the local conference on a basis of local church membership.

Its main purpose is to promote evangelism in its own territory and assist in raising funds for missionary purposes. The local conference entirely supports the pastors of the local churches within its boundaries and has complete charge of assigning and dismissing said pastors. It also has complete charge of every worker within the conference boundaries. It meets once every two years. An executive committee carries on the administrative work in the interim.

The Union Conference

It is composed of an indefinite number of local conferences (depending upon location and conditions). Every local conference president is a delegate to the union conference and other delegates are elected by each local conference according to its membership. Also each union conference worker is a delegate.

An executive board carries on the administrative work.

It meets once every four years. Its main purpose is to supervise and foster work in the different conferences in harmony with the General Conference resolutions and recommendations. It also acts as an advisory organization, and receives reports from the local conferences within its boundaries.

The Division Conference

This is composed of an indefinite number of union conferences (geographic arrangements, e.g., North

America, South America and Southern Africa, etc.). Every division president is a vice-president of the General Conference. It meets once every four years.

All union presidents are delegates and every division conference worker is a delegate to the division conference session. Other delegates are chosen on membership basis.

It has complete general charge of the work in its own territory in harmony with the policies agreed upon at all General Committee meetings, Autumn Councils or General Conference Sessions.

The division conference is governed in its administration by the policies of the General Conference.

The General Conference

This is the international legislative body for the whole world. It meets once every four years. An executive committee handles its affairs in the interim. All members of the General Conference Committee and such members of the division conference committee as are not members of the General Committee, are delegates to the General Conference Session.

It has a Special Council which meets every year and is held in North America. This council is made up of the General Conference Committee, union and local conference presidents of North America, and other division and union conference officials who can attend. This body is legislative in power but its acts are subject to the approval of the General Conference.

CHAPTER V

BAPTISTS

Those adhering to the Baptist doctrines are located, in the order of their numbers in the following places: North America, Europe, Asia, Islands, Africa, South America. Their total number is approximately 1% of the world's and 3% of the total Christian population.

Historical Sketch

The Baptist bodies, as constituted today, trace their origin, as distinct communities, to the Protestant Reformation.

Students of ecclesiastical history cannot fail to notice that the practice of baptizing believers has actually existed since the days of our Lord and his first Apostles.

In the beginning, baptism was administered only to those who could understand the purpose and significance of the sacrament. Sporadically, infant baptism appeared at the end of the second century, and was introduced gradually.

Since 1644 the name has been applied to those who maintain that baptism should be administered to none but believers, and that immersion is the only mode of administering baptism indicated in the New Testament. The doctrine and practices of some earlier bodies, such as the Anabaptists and Mennonites, were similar.

The synod at Carthage (252 A.D.), and the eminent

"church father," Cyprian, are on record as performing infant baptism, but that this was an innovation and not a universal rite is proved by the fact that other church fathers, Augustine, Gregory Naziansen and Chrysostom, all of whom had Christian mothers, were not baptized in infancy. The Emperor Constantine himself, at the end of the third and the beginning of the fourth century, whose mother was the famous Christian woman, Helena, did not receive baptism until he was about to die.

The inference is unavoidable that at this time, baptism as a rule was administered only to believers. Later it became more general, but the exceptions were many, as in the case of the Cathari.

These "Cathari" were quite numerous. The name means the same as our "Puritans." Several sects, as for instance the Bulgari, the Albigenses, Waldenses and others, were called Cathari: They differed among themselves in some doctrines, but they all were opponents of papacy, and many of them were baptists in their administration of baptism.

In southern France, neither the secular arm nor the endeavors of the church could check the growth of the Cathari. In northern Italy, they were counted by the thousands. Alecande III sent a crusading army against the sect in Languedoc (1181-82). At the beginning of the 13th century nearly all the princes and barons of Southern France had embraced their doctrines. Innocent III began a regular war of extirpation in 1208 A.D., during the course of which the sects were scattered. In Spain, France, Flanders and along the Rhine, they suf-

BAPTISTS

fered in the persecution of the Inquisition. A great many of them migrated to the Balkan States.

Thus, history amply testifies to the existence of believers in Christ from the beginning, who, notwithstanding persecution, preserved the original form of baptism. At the time of the reformation by Luther, they had the opportunity to organize themselves and preach their doctrines openly. And this they did, independently of the Anabaptists.

As soon as the Reformation gave men opportunity to interpret the teachings of the Scriptures for themselves, and to embody their convictions in speech and act, persons already holding Baptist doctrines began to appear. In the first quarter of the sixteenth century many were found in Germany and Switzerland, and were called Anabaptists (Re-Baptizers), because they insisted that persons baptized in infancy must, upon profession of conversion, and in order to gain admission into church fellowship, be baptized again, although they do not appear to have insisted always on immersion.

Gradually, in spite of severe persecution, the Baptists grew in numbers. Some of them, driven from Germany, found refuge in the Low Countries and these were gathered, under the lead of Menno Simons, into the groups of Mennonites who passed over into England, and doubtless played an important part in giving currency to Baptist principles.

Glimpses of them appear in the days preceding the Commonwealth; and during the Cromwellian period they became more prominent. It was due to this Mennonite influence that the early Baptist churches in England were Arminian rather than Calvinistic in type, and were termed General Baptists, indicating belief in a universal atonement, in distinction from Particular Baptists, indicating a limited atonement.

In Holland a group of Separatists, led by John Smyth (escaped from persecution in England), came under Mennonite influence and formed in Amsterdam in 1608 the first English Baptist Church, Smyth baptizing first himself, then the others. In 1611 certain of these English Baptists returned to London and established a church there. This was the first of the churches afterward known as General Baptists, since they held the Arminian belief that the atonement of Christ is not limited to the elect only but is general. Particular Baptists were those whose doctrine was Calvinistic, teaching that atonement is particular or individual. The first such church, was formed by secession, in 1638, from a Separatist congregation in Southwark, London. Immersion was not yet insisted upon in these churches; but in 1644 seven Particular Baptist churches issued a Confession of Faith requiring that form of baptism, and Baptist was thenceforth the name given to those who practiced it. A general assembly of General Baptist churches was formed in 1671; of Particular Baptist churches, in 1689. In 1891 General and Particular Baptists united. It was the Particular type that first took root among the Puritans and Calvinists in America, when Roger Williams and his companions in Rhode Island rejected infant baptism and established a church in 1639. The church of Newport was organized at about the same time. Baptists were later persecuted in New England for not having children baptized, and one group emigrated from Maine to Charleston, S. C., in 1684. In the Southeast the General Baptist views found acceptance, but the stricter Calvinistic ideas suited the pioneers who settled the southern mountains after the Revolution. Their opposition to mission work gave them the name Anti-Mission. They were also called Hard Shell, Old School, or Primitive Baptists. In 1788 the first Colored Baptist Church was organized.

The Baptists are today scattered over the whole world. They afford an extremely variegated picture. This picture was of course much simplified in the earlier days in England, when different groups joined together to form the Baptist Union. There are, on the other hand, eighteen Baptist bodies in the United States. The reason for the divisions in the United States is partly due to the dogmatic differences arising between the congregations who held predestination and universalistic views. Besides, there are the "Seventh-day Baptists," who deviate from the others on account of their observing Saturday as the Sabbath Day, instead of Sunday. Besides this cultus deviation, there is the difference arising from the variety of viewpoints due to sectionalism. Thus arises the distinction between the Northern and Southern Baptist Convention. The race question, as with other Protestant denominations, plays a role; and there are a number of independent Negro churches.

The history of the early Baptist churches in New England is one of constant struggle for existence. The Puritan government of Massachusetts was so bitter in its opposition that nearly a century after Roger Williams there were but eight Baptist churches in that colony. Conditions elsewhere were similar, although farther south there was less persecution.

With the general emancipation from ecclesiastical rule that followed the Revolutionary War, all disabilities were removed from the Baptists in the different states, and the new Federal Constitution effaced the last vestige of religious inequality.

As the discussion in regard to slavery became acute, there arose the differences which resulted in the present three conventions—Northern, Southern, and National. The southern churches withdrew in 1845 and formed the Southern Baptist Convention, whose purpose was to do for the Southern Baptist churches just what the general convention had hitherto done for the entire Baptist denomination. It was not a new denomination, but simply a new organization for the direction of the missionary and general evangelistic work of the churches of the Southern states.

These early American Baptist churches belonged to the Particular, or Calvinistic branch. Later, Arminian views became widely spread for a time, but ultimately the Calvinistic view of the atonement was generally accepted by the main body of Baptists in the Colonies. The divisions which now exist began to make their appearance at a relatively early date. Arminianism practically disappeared from the Baptist churches of New England about the middle of the eighteenth century, but General Baptists were found in Virginia before 1714, and this branch gained a permanent foothold in the South.

Soon after the Revolutionary War, the question of

the evangelization of the Negro race assumed importance, and a Colored Baptist church was organized in 1788.

As missionary work became organized into societies, many of these associations opposed, not so much mission work itself, as its organization, through fear of a developing ecclesiasticism. These were variously termed "Old School," "Anti-Mission," "Hard Shell," and "Primitive" Baptists; but gradually the term "Primitive" became the most widely known and adopted. In contradistinction to these, the association, or churches, which approved of missionary societies, came to be designated Missionary Baptists, though there was no definite denominational organization under that name.

The denominations mentioned, however, do not represent all who hold Baptist views, for during the revival period just referred to the Disciples of Christ, or Churches of Christ, arose. In practice they are essentially Baptists, although they differ from the other bodies in some interpretations. With them also may be classed the Adventists, the Brethren (Dunker, Plymouth, and River) Mennonites, and certain other bodies. The Armenian and Eastern Orthodox Churches practice baptism by immersion, but do not limit it to those of mature years.

By far the largest body of Baptists, not only in the United States, but in the world, is that popularly known as "Baptists," though frequently referred to as "Regular Baptists." Other Baptist bodies prefix some descriptive adjective, such as "Primitive," "United," "General," "Free Will," etc.; but this, which is virtually the parent body, commonly has no such qualifications. Its churches, however, are ordinarily spoken of as "Northern," "Southern," and "National," or "Colored." This does not imply any radical divergence in doctrine or ecclesiastical order. All are essentially one in these respects, and the division into the three major groups is largely for administrative purposes.

Doctrine

It is a distinctive principle with Baptists that they acknowledge no human founder, recognize no human authority, and subscribe to no human creed. For all these things, Baptists of every name and order go back to the New Testament. While no competent Baptist historian presumes to be able to trace a succession of Baptist churches through the ages, most of them are of one accord in believing that, if we could secure the records, there would be found heroic groups of believers in every age who upheld with their testimonies, and in many cases with their lives, the great outstanding and distinctive principles of the Baptist churches of today.

The cardinal principle of Baptists is implicit obedience to the plain teachings of the Word of God. Under this principle, while maintaining with other evangelical bodies the great truths of the Christian religion, they hold: (1) That the churches are independent in their local affairs; (2) that there should be an entire separation of Church and state; (3) that religious liberty or freedom in matters of religion is an inherent right of the human soul; (4) that a church is a body of regenerated people who have been baptized on profession of personal faith in Christ, and have associated themselves in the fellowship of the gospel; (5) that infant baptism is not only not taught in the Scriptures, but is fatal to the spirituality of the church; (6) that from the meaning of the word used in the Greek text of the Scriptures, the symbolism of the ordinance, and the practice of the early church, immersion in water is the only proper mode of baptism; (7) that the scriptural officers of a church are pastors and deacons; and (8) that the Lord's Supper is an ordinance of the church observed in commemoration of the sufferings and death of Christ.

The beliefs of Baptists have been incorporated in confessions of faith. Of these, the Philadelphia Confession, originally issued by the London Baptist churches in 1689, and adopted with some enlargements by the Philadelphia Association in 1742, and the New Hampshire Confession, in 1832, are recognized as the most important, for Baptists in America. But while these confessions are recognized as fair expressions of faith of Baptists, there is nothing binding in them, and they are not regarded as having any special authority. The final court of appeal for Baptists is the Word of God. Within limits, considerable differences in doctrine are allowed, and thus opportunity is given to modify beliefs as new light may break from or upon the "Word." Among Baptists, heresy trials are rare, thus indicating the latitude of individual interpretation of doctrine.

Divisions of the Baptists

The following churches, although they are distinctly separate bodies, have doctrines and governments substantially the same:

Seventh-day Baptists, London, organized 1617; Free Baptists; General Six Principle Baptists, organized 1653; Free Will Baptist, Wales, organized 1701; Brethren (German Baptist Dunkers); Church of the Brethren, Germany, organized 1708; General Baptists, Virginia, organized 1714; National Baptists Convention (Colored), Georgia, organized 1778; Free Will Baptist (Bullockites), organized 1780, New Hampshire; Separate Baptists, Virginia, organized 1787; United Baptists, Virginia, organized 1794; Colored Primitive Baptists; Two-Seed-in-the-Spirit, Tennessee, organized 1806 (Predestinarian Baptists); Duck River and Kindred Ass'ns. of Baptists (Baptist Church of Christ), Kentucky, organized 1808; Primitive Baptists, North Carolina, 1827; Colored Free Will Baptists, 1901, North Carolina; Primitive Baptists (Progressive); Regular Baptists; Southern Baptist Convention, organized 1845; Northern Baptist Convention, organized 1907.

Main Divisions

Northern Baptist Convention

History. After the withdrawal of the Southern churches, 1845, the Baptist churches of the North continued to grow. The intense controversies of the eighteenth century and the early part of the nineteenth century were no longer manifest. Educational institutions developed, and there came to be a general unity of purpose and of life. The individualism which distinguished earlier times gradually gave place to a closer associationalism. Various organizations which had already proved their value elsewhere were adopted into the denominational life, all tending toward mutual church action. The Young People's Union rallied the forces of the young people, both for church life and general denominational activity. The Baptist Congress was formed for the consideration of matters affecting the general welfare of the churches.

The chief change in denominational methods of late years was the organization of the Northern Baptist Convention, at Washington, D. C., in 1907, as a strictly delegated body for the Baptist churches of the North and West. The three great denominational societies, including the separate societies of women, have placed themselves under its direction, and report each year to the convention.

The Northern churches are less rigidly Calvinistic in their doctrine than the Southern churches. Membership and ministry are interchanged on terms of perfect equality. In the Northern Convention, the dividing line between the white and negro churches is not as sharply drawn as in the Southern. There are negro members of white churches, and negro churches in white associations, while white and negro associations mingle more freely.

Southern Baptist Convention

History. At the time of the formation of the Triennial Convention in 1814, the Baptist population was chiefly in New England and the Middle and Southern seaboard states, and the center of executive administration was located first at Philadelphia and subsequently at Boston. With the growth of migration to the South and Southwest, the number of churches in those sections of the country greatly increased, and it became difficult to associate in a single advisory council more than a small percentage of the Baptist churches in the United States, especially since means of transportation were deficient and expensive. At the same time, the question of slavery occasioned much discussion between the two sections.

This led to formal withdrawal of the various Southern state conventions and auxiliary foreign mission societies, and to the organization at Augusta, Ga., in May, 1845, of the Southern Baptist Convention. About 300 churches were represented. In all the discussions and in the final act of organization, there was very little bitterness, the prevalent conviction being that those of kindred thought would work more effectively together.

Negro Baptists

There are over three million Negro Baptists in America. Prior to 1895, they were organized into various separate denominations, which in that year were brought together in what is known as the National Baptist Convention. They have subsequently divided themselves into three divisions, due to differences in organization and work.

There have been various attempts to re-unite these factions, but as yet they have been unsuccessful. All conform to the Northern and Southern Baptists Conventions in doctrine.

Organization and Government

Baptist church governments and organizations are congregational or independent. They organize free congregations and avoid graduated hierarchical systems. Baptist churches are congregational in matters of government. Such general associations as are formed do not have control over the individual churches. The first union of the whole body in England, at the end of the 18th century, was for missionary activities. By missions the Baptist movement was extended to the Continent. The organization for mission work thus begun was incorporated in 1900 as the Baptist Union for Great Britain and Ireland. In the United States the American Baptist Missionary Union (under a longer title) was formed in 1814 to support workers in foreign lands. When the question of slavery became a dividing wall, the Southern Baptist Convention was established, 1845, with its various boards for missions and other activities. The Northern Baptist Convention, organized in 1907, is a delegated body operating through many agencies. Both support a number of educational institutions and periodicals. The original national organization of the Negro Baptist churches is the National Baptist Convention of the United States of America. Separated from this body in 1915 is the National Baptist Convention of America. The four principal conventions agree in doctrine and ecclesiastical order. Other groups have their own associations, among them the conservative American Baptist Association of the Southwest, sometimes called "Landmarkers," organized in 1905; the Free Baptists, whose

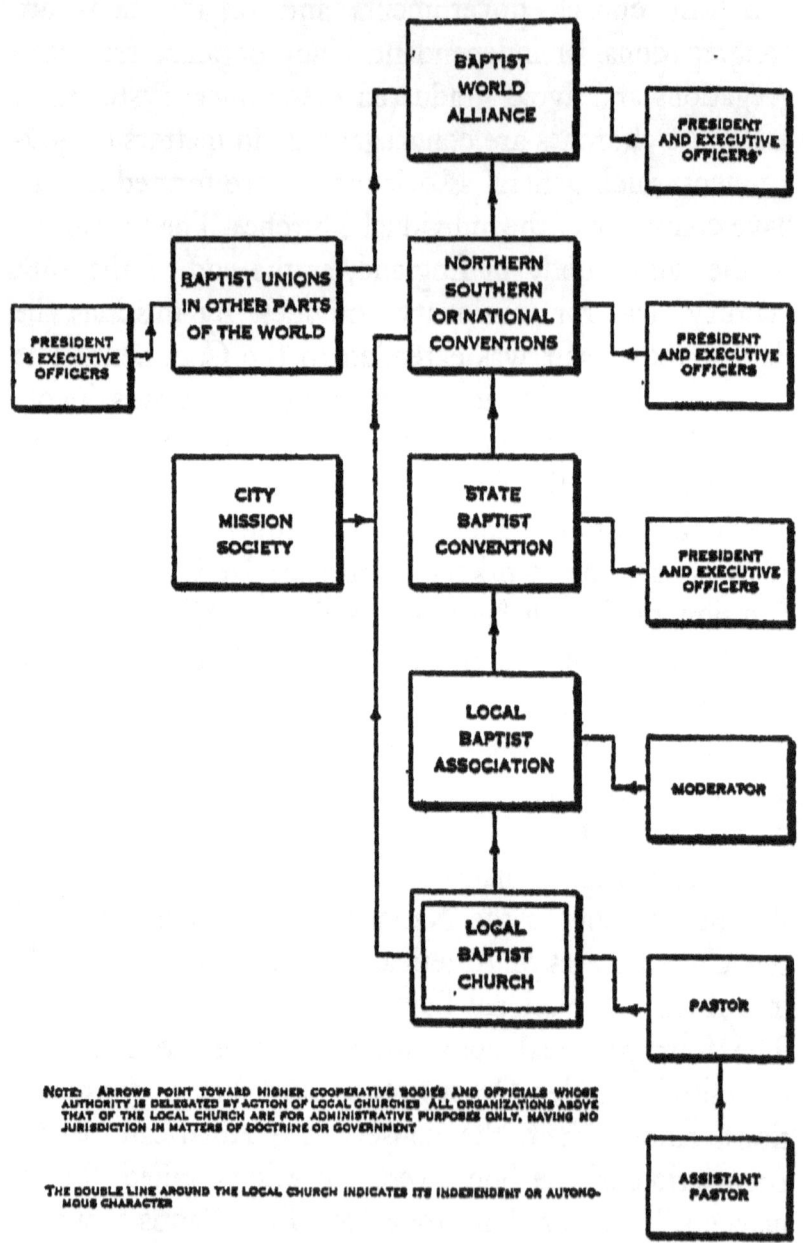

General Convention dates from 1826; the Seventh-Day Baptists; Duck River Baptists, Free Will Baptists; etc. There are no fewer than 19 bodies.

Each church is sovereign so far as its own discipline and worship are concerned, calls or dismisses its own pastor, elects its own deacons or other officers, and attends to its own affairs. Admission to church membership is by vote of the church, usually after examination of the candidate by the church committee. There is no specific age limit, although the admission of very young children is discouraged. All members have equal voting rights in church matters, except that in some churches they are restricted to those over a certain age. The officers are the pastor and deacons, who, with such other persons as the church may elect, constitute a church committee, usually called the standing committee, and have general care of the affairs of the church, but no authority, except as it is specifically delegated to them by the church. Church property is held sometimes by a board of trustees, sometimes by the entire society, and sometimes by a special committee of the church.

Applicants for the ministry are licensed to preach by the church in which they hold membership. If after a period of service as licentiate, ordination is desired, a council of sister churches is called by the church in which membership is held, and on the recommendation of this council the church arranges for ordination. In both cases the right to license and the right to ordain are held by the individual church. Previous to ordination there is always an examination of the candidate on matters of religious experience, call to the ministry, and views of scriptural doctrine. During his ministry, a pastor is usually a member of the church which he serves, and is amenable to its discipline. When a question of dismissal from the ministry arises, the individual church calls a council of sister churches for the examination of charges, and on the recommendation of this council, the church usually bases its decision.

Besides local associations, Baptists have also organized state conventions or state mission societies, state educational societies, city mission societies, etc. These larger bodies attend to missionary or educational work in the various states or districts, and are supported by the churches. In some states there are two or more of these general bodies.

There are also general or national organizations for missionary, publication or educational purposes. Like the local associations, none of these larger organizations has any authority over the individual churches.

The Local Church

    Consists of the following:

        Pastor
        Board of Deacons
        Board of Deaconesses (may have)
        Board of Trustees
        Church Clerk
        Financial Secretary ⎫
        Treasurer   ⎬ (May be combined)
        Sunday School Superintendent

BAPTISTS

Men's Organizations
Young People's Organizations
Women's Auxiliary
Mission Circles

Each local church is sovereign and autonomous in all its affairs. All other organizations with a broader scope are for administrative purposes only.

Each local church appoints one delegate for each one hundred members and an additional delegate for each additional one hundred members or major fraction thereof, to the Northern, Southern, or National Convention (depending upon the convention to which the local church belongs).

Local Baptist Association

For missionary and educational or other purposes, Baptist churches usually group themselves into local associations. These associations meet annually and are composed of messengers sent by the churches. They elect their own officers, receive reports from the churches, and make recommendations with regard to work or other matters in which the churches are interested. They have, however, no authority to legislate for the churches, and no power to enforce any action they may take. Many of them conduct missionary or educational work in the fields covered by them.

The State Baptist Convention

Each local church, desiring to cooperate, appoints two delegates for each one hundred members and one additional delegate for each additional one hundred members or major fraction thereof, to the State Baptist Convention.

The State Baptist Convention meets once a year. A Board of Trustees, members of which are elected alternately for a three-year term, acts as the executive head of the State Baptist Convention.

The main purpose of this convention is to conduct missions within its boundaries and for general dispensing of local information and administrative purposes.

The Northern, The Southern and The National Baptist Conventions (Separate Organizations)

Each local church, belonging to either of the three above titles, sends delegates on the basis of one delegate for each one hundred members and an additional delegate for every additional one hundred members or major fraction thereof, to the convention to which it belongs.

Each of the three national organizations meets separately each year. Each has an executive committee for purposes of administrative operations, and each organization functions and operates entirely separate of the others.

Baptist Unions in Other Parts of the World

They are similar in their autonomous character as are the Northern and Southern Baptist Conventions in the United States.

The Baptist World Alliance

It consists of representatives from conventions or associations or unions of Baptist churches throughout the world. The officers consist of a president, seven vice-presidents, a correspondent from every country represented, a general secretary, an honorary secretary, and a treasurer from each hemisphere.

The Baptist World Alliance meets in general meeting ordinarily once in five years.

An executive committee composed of the president, past presidents, vice-presidents, secretaries, treasurers, and twenty-nine other members, of whom four shall be from Great Britain, nine from the United States of America, two from Canada, and ten from other countries, acts as the administrative head.

The main purpose of the Alliance is to show the essential oneness of Baptist people in the Lord Jesus Christ, to impart inspiration to the brotherhood, and to promote the spirit of fellowship, service, and cooperation among its members while recognizing the independence of each particular church.

CHAPTER VI

CHURCH OF CHRIST, SCIENTIST

Those adhering to the Christian Science doctrines are located the world over but principally in the United States, British Empire, and Germany. The Christian Scientists do not engage in missionary work as other denominations do.

HISTORICAL SKETCH

Christian Science is the religion founded by Mary Baker Eddy and represented by the Church of Christ, Scientist. The Christian Science denomination was founded by Mrs. Eddy at Boston in 1879, following her discovery of this religion at Lynn, Mass., in 1866, and her issuing of its textbook, *Science and Health with Key to the Scriptures*, in 1875.

For many years prior to 1866, Mrs. Eddy observed and studied mental causes and effects. Profoundly religious, she was disposed to attribute causation to God and to regard Him as divine Mind. At Lynn, Mass., in that year, she recovered almost instantly from a severe injury, after reading an account of healing in the Gospel according to St. Matthew. The discovery which she named "Christian Science" ensued from this incident.

At first, Mrs. Eddy did not expect to found a distinct church or denomination; she hoped that her restoration to original Christianity of its healing power would be accepted by existing churches, as her teachings and the results of their practice became known. In a few years, however, it became evident that a distinct church was needed to facilitate cooperation and unity between Christian Scientists, to present Christian Science to all people, and to maintain the purity of its teachings and practice.

Accordingly, she and her followers organized the Church of Christ, Scientist, "to commemorate the words and works of our Master which should re-instate primitive Christianity and its lost element of healing."

Mrs. Eddy passed on in 1910. Until then, she had initiated every step in the progress of Christian Science. Nothing of moment was done without her approval. Although the organic law of the Christian Science movement through its Church Manual, confers extensive and sufficient powers upon an administrative board—The Christian Science Board of Directors—nevertheless it had always functioned under her immediate supervision. Mrs. Eddy's demise, therefore, immediately tested the adequacy of the Church Manual as an organic law and the loyalty of Christian Scientists to this law, in the absence of its author.

The primary source of information about Christian Science is Mrs. Eddy's book, *Science and Health with Key to the Scriptures*, first published in 1875 and occasionally revised, "only to give a clearer and fuller expression of its original meaning." This book received from the author its final revision in 1907. Mrs. Eddy was the author of numerous other books on Christian Science, published from 1886 to 1913.

Doctrine

The theology of Christian Science begins with the proposition that God is the only might or Mind; that He "is incorporeal, divine, supreme, infinite Mind, Spirit, Soul, Principle, Life, Truth, Love;" that He is the "divine Principle of all that really is." To define God further, it employs frequently the word "good," besides such terms as Life, Truth, Love. Next to God, the name of Jesus and reference to him occur most frequently in the authorized literature of Christian Science.

Concerning Jesus Christ and his relation to God and man, Christian Science distinguishes between what is in the New Testament and what is in the creeds, doctrines, and dogmas of later times. Accordingly, Christian Scientists speak of him oftenest as the "Way" or the "Way-shower," and they regard the atonement, his chief work, as "the exemplification of man's unity with God, whereby man reflects divine Truth, Life and Love."

The most distinctive feature of Christian Science teaching is its absolute distinction between what is real and what is apparent or seeming, but unreal. This distinction Mrs. Eddy explains, for instance, as follows: "All reality is in God and His creation, harmonious and eternal. That which He creates is good, and He makes all that is made. Therefore the only reality of sin, sickness, or death is the awful fact that unrealities seem real to human, erring belief, until God strips off their disguise. They are not true, because they are not of God."

Contrary to common misapprehension, Christian Science does not ignore what it regards as unreal. This

CHURCH OF CHRIST, SCIENTIST

religion teaches its adherents to forsake and overcome every form of error or evil on the basis of its unreality; that is, by demonstrating the true idea of reality. This it teaches them to do by means of spiritual law and spiritual power.

In this connection, Christian Science maintains that the truth of being—the truth concerning God and man—includes a rule for its practice and a law by which its practice produces effects. Jesus declared this rule and law when he said, "Ye shall know the truth, and the truth shall make you free" (John viii, 32). Accordingly, for an individual to gain his freedom from any form of error or evil, he should know the truth, the absolute truth of being, applicable to his case; and Christian Science further teaches that this practice is effective when employed by one individual for another, because such is the unity of real being and such is the law of God. For these reasons, evidently, Jesus could and did declare the possibility of spiritual healing in unlimited terms.

The practice of Christian Science is not merely mental; it must be also spiritual. Indeed, it is truly mental only as it is absolutely spiritual. The non-spiritual elements in the so-called human mind do not contribute to harmony or to health. The practitioner must know or realize spiritually, and his ability to do this is derived from the divine Mind. Therefore, he must agree with the Teacher and Way-shower, who said, "I can of mine own self do nothing" (John v, 30), and he must prepare for the healing ministry and keep himself in condition for it by living the life of a genuine Christian.

The practice of Christian Science is not limited, as is

commonly supposed, to the healing of the sick. On the contrary, Christian Scientists regard their religion as applicable to every human need, including the destruction of sin in mortal thought.

Organization and Government

Since its reorganization in 1892, the denomination has consisted of The Christian Science Mother Church, the proper name of which is The First Church of Christ, Scientist, in Boston, Mass., and branch churches or branch societies at all places where there are enough adherents for a local organization. A branch church is called First Church of Christ, Scientist, of its city or town, or is called Second Church of Christ, Scientist, of that place and so on. A society is the beginning of a church, and is called Christian Science Society of its locality.

Viewed in another way, The Mother Church consists of members who constitute the local congregation in Boston and of members who reside in other places throughout the world and who may or may not also be a member of a branch church or society.

The officers of The Mother Church consist of The Christian Science Board of Directors, President, First and Second Readers, Clerk, and Treasurer.

The Lesson-Sermon which constitutes the principal part of the service, is prepared by a committee connected with The Mother Church and is read in every Christian Science Church or Society by two readers, who read alternately, the Second Reader from the Bible, and the First Reader from the Christian Science textbook,

CHURCH OF CHRIST, SCIENTIST

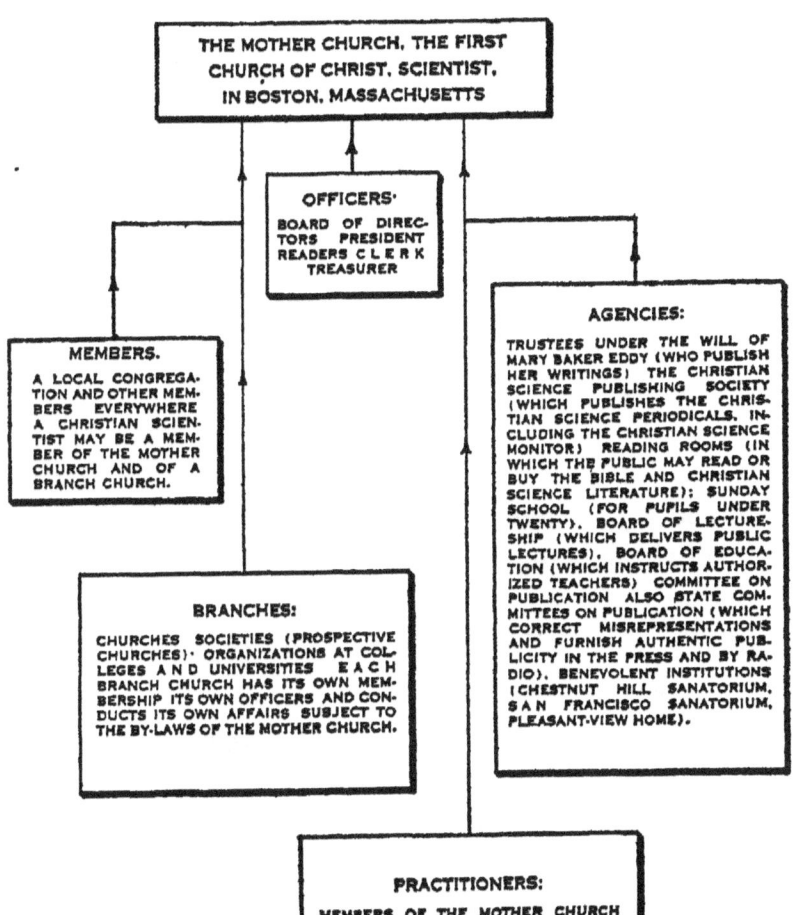

Science and Health with Key to the Scriptures by Mary Baker Eddy.

A Wednesday evening testimony meeting is likewise conducted by the First Reader who reads appropriate selections from the Bible and correlative passages from the Christian Science textbook. Time is provided at these meetings for testimonies by those in attendance who have been healed and regenerated through the study and application of the teachings of Christian Science.

All of the activities of the Christian Science denomination are intended to promote spiritualization of thought, together with the innumerable results thereof, which include spiritual healing. In the healing of the sick, practiced for the benefit of particular persons, the service rendered by healers or practitioners is regarded as an individual ministry, subject only to a degree of regulation by the Church.

Membership in The Mother Church is limited to those applicants who are at least twelve years of age; not members of any other denomination; of Christian character; and who believe in and have some understanding of Christian Science according to the teachings and tenets in its textbook, *Science and Health with Key to the Scriptures*. The age limit for membership in branch churches or societies varies; otherwise the same qualifications are prerequisites.

CHAPTER VII

CHURCH OF JESUS CHRIST OF LATTER-DAY SAINTS
(Mormon)

Those adhering to the Latter-day Saints' doctrines are located principally in the United States, particularly in the Western States. Missionary work is carried on in practically all foreign countries.

Historical Sketch

The Church of Jesus Christ of Latter-day Saints is the proper name of the body of religious people commonly known as "Mormons." Its adherents maintain it was brought about by the authority and commandment of God. It was organized in the State of New York on the sixth day of April, eighteen-hundred-thirty, and derives all its doctrines, ordinances, discipline and orders of Priesthood from direct, divine revelation.

Joseph Smith became the first prophet and president of the Church. In the year 1820, when but fourteen years of age and while living in Manchester, Ontario County, New York, he had, as he afterwards related, in the woods near his father's home, a vision of great light, and two glorious personages, God the Father and Jesus Christ the Son, appeared before him and commanded him "to join none of the religious sects, for the Lord was about to restore the gospel, which was not represented in its fulness by any of the existing churches." Other visions followed, and in one he received directions enabling him to obtain "the sacred records, an abridgment of the history kept by the ancient inhabitants of America" which "were engraven on plates which had the appearance of gold." These records, constituting the "Book of Mormon," he translated, dictating the translation to Oliver Cowdery. Mr. Cowdery, David Whitmer and Martin Harris, after the completion of the work gave their testimony that they had actually seen the plates.

Joseph Smith and Oliver Cowdery stated that in May, 1829, "an angel, John the Baptist, appeared to them and conferred upon them the priesthood of Aaron and instructed them to baptize each other by immersion."

This visitation was followed, in April, 1830, by the organization of the Church at Fayette, New York, and "the declaration that the ancient gospel had been restored with all its gifts and powers."

Other visitations of heavenly messengers were received through which authority and enlightenment on the true Gospel of Jesus Christ were bestowed and imparted to the young prophet and his associate Oliver Cowdery.

Missionaries were sent out and numerous branches were organized in various states. In 1831, headquarters were established at Kirtland, Ohio. From the first, the policy of establishing the converts in communities of their own was followed, and in 1831 a colony of believers was settled in Jackson County, Missouri. Here they met violent opposition from neighbors, which culminated, in 1833, in their being driven from the county by mob violence. They then were forced to scatter into other counties, although retaining their organization at Kirtland, Ohio; and in 1838 Joseph Smith, with other leaders, removed to Caldwell County, Missouri, which was settled almost exclusively by Latter-day Saints. Then followed the settlement at Nauvoo, Hancock County, Illinois, which developed rapidly, and at one time was the largest city in the state. In a few years, however, the people of the surrounding counties became hostile, and Joseph Smith and his brother Hyrum were killed by a mob at Carthage, Illinois, on the 27th of June, 1844.

After the death of Joseph Smith, Brigham Young, as president of the Council of the Twelve Apostles, was chosen president of the Church, and three years later led a general migration of the Church from Illinois to the Great Salt Lake Valley, which later became part of the State of Utah, and which is the present headquarters of the Church of Jesus Christ of Latter-day Saints.

Prior to the "exodus" of the Church from Illinois to the Rocky Mountains, a few became dissatisfied with the succession of Brigham Young and the Quorum of the Twelve Apostles to the leadership of the Church and remained behind. They formed into several small groups under various leaders.

In 1852 Jason W. Briggs and Zenas H. Gurley gathered some of the scattered remnants of these groups and formed what they called the "New Organization of the Church" and began to preach the doctrine of the "rejection" of the Church of Jesus Christ of Latter-day Saints because they said the saints had failed to build the temple at Nauvoo within a given time which expired at or shortly following the death of Joseph and Hyrum Smith, and therefore it became necessary to reorganize that they might find favor with the Lord.

They also promulgated the doctrine of "lineal priesthood" claiming that it was the right of the oldest son of Joseph Smith to succeed his father in the presidency of the Church. For a number of years they labored to induce Joseph Smith, son of the Prophet, to take the presidency of the new organization, but without success. Finally at a conference held in Amboy, Ill. in April 1860 he consented and was installed as president of the new organization which was later incorporated as the "Reorganized Church of Jesus Christ of Latter-day Saints." Some of the doctrines they rejected were Polygamy, the building of temples and the living doing work for the dead.

Their members are located principally around the middle western states with headquarters at Independence, Mo. Total membership is approximately 90,000.

The comparative isolation of the new location gave less occasion for such disturbances as had theretofore accompanied the Church, and permitted a more normal development of community life. From this point, Salt Lake City, as a center, the church, through its missionary activities has been extended to every state in the United States and to practically all foreign countries, and the number of converts has increased rapidly. Brigham Young died in 1877, and was followed, in succession, by John Taylor, Wilford Woodruff, Lorenzo Snow, Joseph F. Smith and Heber J. Grant (present head of the Church).

Doctrine

According to ecclesiastical history, the Apostles appointed by Christ to establish His church on earth were slain. Their immediate successors and a great number of their disciples were also slain or tortured, and gradually darkness came over the world and pagan institutions were mingled with the rites and order of the Church, until the apostolic authority and the true Christian spirit and doctrine were entirely subverted. Reforms that were subsequently introduced merely lopped off some evils and made some improvements; but did not and could not restore the authority and power of the primitive Christian Church and Priesthood.

In these latter days, God the Father and Jesus Christ the Son have appeared and revealed anew the Gospel. Angels have ministered to man. John the Baptist brought to earth the authority of the lesser or Aaronic Priesthood, which he held when in mortality. Peter, James, and John conferred their keys of Apostleship and the power and authority of the higher or Melchizedek Priesthood on men of this generation. Elijah, the Prophet, and others of the ancients have bestowed the keys they held, and these are all in the Church of Jesus Christ of Latter-day Saints. Under that authority the Church has been built up after the original pattern and with the same spirit, ordinances, gifts and blessings.

Joseph Smith was the instrument in the hands of the Lord to commence the work of restitution, and open the last dispensation, that of the "fulness of times." He received that divine authority under the hands of those heavenly messengers. He, by revelation and commandment, ordained others. Today there are on earth Apostles, Prophets, Evangelists, High Priests, Elders, Bishops, Priests, Teachers and Deacons, divinely called and authorized to teach and administer the things of the Kingdom of Heaven, and the power of God attends their administrations.

Faith, repentance, and baptism in water and by the Spirit, administered by divine authority, are essential to salvation. There is but one way. There is some good in all religions, but there is and can be but one divine religion, and that is, the Gospel of Christ. Infants who die before they become accountable need no baptism but are redeemed by the blood of Christ.

The spirit of man is an intelligent, responsible being, an entity both before and after dwelling in the body. It was in the beginning with the Father. The sons and daughters of God, after probation in the flesh, return to Him and then, until the resurrection, associate in such sphere as they have fitted themselves to occupy—the good with the spirits of the just, the evil with the spirits of the unjust. A disembodied spirit can learn, believe, repent and yield obedience, but cannot be baptized in water, the earthly medium of purification—hence the necessity of properly administered baptism here on earth.

The living may be baptized for the dead. One who has received the ordinances of the Gospel can stand proxy for departed ancestors, who, on obedience to the Gospel in the spirit, will receive the benefit of the earthly ordinances. As the spirit of Christ preached to the spirits in prison while His body was in the sepulchre, so His servants, bearing His authority, preach to "the dead," after having finished their work on earth. Ordinances for and in behalf of the dead are administered in Temples built and maintained especially for this sacred service.

The resurrection of Jesus of Nazareth was "the firstfruits of them that slept." All persons who have breathed the breath of life will also be raised from the dead, receiving their bodies again, as did He. Everyone in his own order and degree of perfection, depending on the life led here upon the earth, will be judged according to his works. Eventually, all who can be saved will be placed in some degree of glory and advancement.

The Book of Mormon does not take the place of the Bible, but is auxiliary to it and corroborates and supports it. The Bible is the record of God's dealings with His people on the Eastern Continent; the Book of Mormon is the record of God's dealings with His people on the Western Continent, separated from the other hemisphere and long unknown to its inhabitants. These two records, together with the book of Doctrine and Covenants (containing modern revelations) and the Pearl of Great Price, are the standards of doctrine and discipline of the Church.

What the ancient Hebrew prophets and apostles wrote or spoke through the inspiration of the Holy Spirit, the Latter-day Saints accept as divine revelation.

Revelation conveys the word and will of God. Every individual in the Church is entitled to it for his or her own guidance. The President of the Church, who is a prophet, a seer and a revelator, is entitled to divine communication by any of the means which God chooses to use for this purpose. But revelation does not come by the will of man. It is God who reveals His word at the time and in the manner which He selects. Revelation for the whole Church comes through the head alone, and thus, order is preserved and conflicting doctrines excluded.

The doctrine of eternal marriage is a feature of the "Mormon" faith. By the authority vested in the head of the Church, that which is sealed on earth is sealed in heaven, and the man and woman united under that authority, as an everlasing covenant, are joined forever.

The family, the home, the relations of parents and children, are thus the basis of present and future happiness; and the increase thereof is eternal.

The first principle of the Gospel of Jesus Christ as taught by this Church is faith. This means faith in God the Father and in His Son Jesus Christ and in the Holy Ghost.

The Father (God) is a glorified and perfected personage, and Jesus Christ, the Son is in His (God's) express image and likeness. One is an individual as much as the other (separate personages). Each is a spirit clothed with a spiritual, yet tangible, immortal body. Spirit is substance, not immateriality. It is eternal in its essence, and so are the ultimate elements of that which is known as matter.

Man is a dual being, also in the image of God, who is the Father of his spirit and the Creator of his body. Jesus was the First-born in the spirit and the Only-begotten in the flesh. All men and women are the sons and daughters of God, and Jesus is their elder brother.

Baptism is the third principle, and its mode is immersion in water in the likeness of a burial, succeeded by a resurrection; it is also symbolical of a birth. Becoming dead to sin by repentance, the believer is buried in the liquid grave and brought forth from the womb of water; thus he is "born" of water to a new life in Christ Jesus.

The fourth principle is the bestowal of the Holy Ghost by the laying on of hands, by men called and ordained of God to thus officiate in His name.

No person has the right to baptize, or lay on hands, or administer an ordinance of the Church, unless he is called of God and ordained to act in His name. The commission given to the Apostles of old does not confer any authority upon men in this age. It was for those alone upon whom it was bestowed, and those whom they were inspired and directed to ordain unto the same power. Without divine communication now, there can be no divine authority today.

In concise summary, the Articles of Faith of the Church of Jesus Christ of Latter-day Saints are proclaimed as follows:

1. We believe in God, the Eternal Father, and in His Son, Jesus Christ, and in the Holy Ghost.
2. We believe that men will be punished for their own sins, and not for Adam's transgression.
3. We believe that through the Atonement of Christ all mankind may be saved, by obedience to the laws and ordinances of the Gospel.
4. We believe that the first principles and ordinances of the Gospel are: first, Faith in the Lord Jesus Christ;

second, Repentance; third, Baptism by immersion for the remission of sins; fourth, Laying on of hands for the gift of the Holy Ghost.

5. We believe that a man must be called of God, by prophecy, and by the laying on of hands by those who are in authority, to preach the Gospel and administer in the ordinances thereof.

6. We believe in the same organization that existed in the Primitive Church, viz., apostles, prophets, pastors, teachers, evangelists, etc.

7. We believe in the gift of tongues, prophecy, revelation, visions, healing, interpretation of tongues, etc.

8. We believe the Bible to be the word of God as far as it is translated correctly; we also believe the Book of Mormon to be the word of God.

9. We believe all that God has revealed, all that He does now reveal, and we believe that He will yet reveal many great and important things pertaining to the Kingdom of God.

10. We believe in the literal gathering of Israel and in the restoration of the Ten Tribes; that Zion will be built upon this (the American) continent; that Christ will reign personally upon the earth; and, that the earth will be renewed and receive its paradisical glory.

11. We claim the privilege of worshipping Almighty God according to the dictates of our own conscience, and allow all men the same privilege, let them worship how, where, or what they may.

12. We believe in being subject to kings, presidents, rulers, and magistrates, in obeying, honoring, and sustaining the law.

13. We believe in being honest, true, chaste, benevolent, virtuous, and in doing good to all men; indeed, we may say that we follow the admonition of Paul—We believe all things, we hope all things, we have endured many things, and hope to be able to endure all things. If there is anything virtuous, lovely, or of good report or praiseworthy, we seek after these things.—Joseph Smith.

The great distinctive feature of "Mormonism" among the "Christian" denominations is its claim of direct, divine origin. Present and continuous revelation from God to the Church through its earthly head, and to every member who seeks for it in his or her own behalf and guidance, is a fundamental principle of the faith.

Organization and Government

The Church of Jesus Christ of Latter-day Saints maintains that its organization is similar to the organization of the Church of Christ which was extant during and shortly after Christ's earthly life, but which subsequently, because of the great apostacy, became extinct.

The Church is organized "for the perfecting of the Saints, for the work of the ministry, for the edifying of the body of Christ; till we all come in unity of the faith, and of the knowledge of the Son of God."

Any organization, religious or political, should be endowed with the authority necessary to carry out its purposes. A true church of Christ must have, inherent in it, the power and authority to act in His name. The Church of Jesus Christ of Latter-day Saints was organized, and is now directed, by "men called of God" and

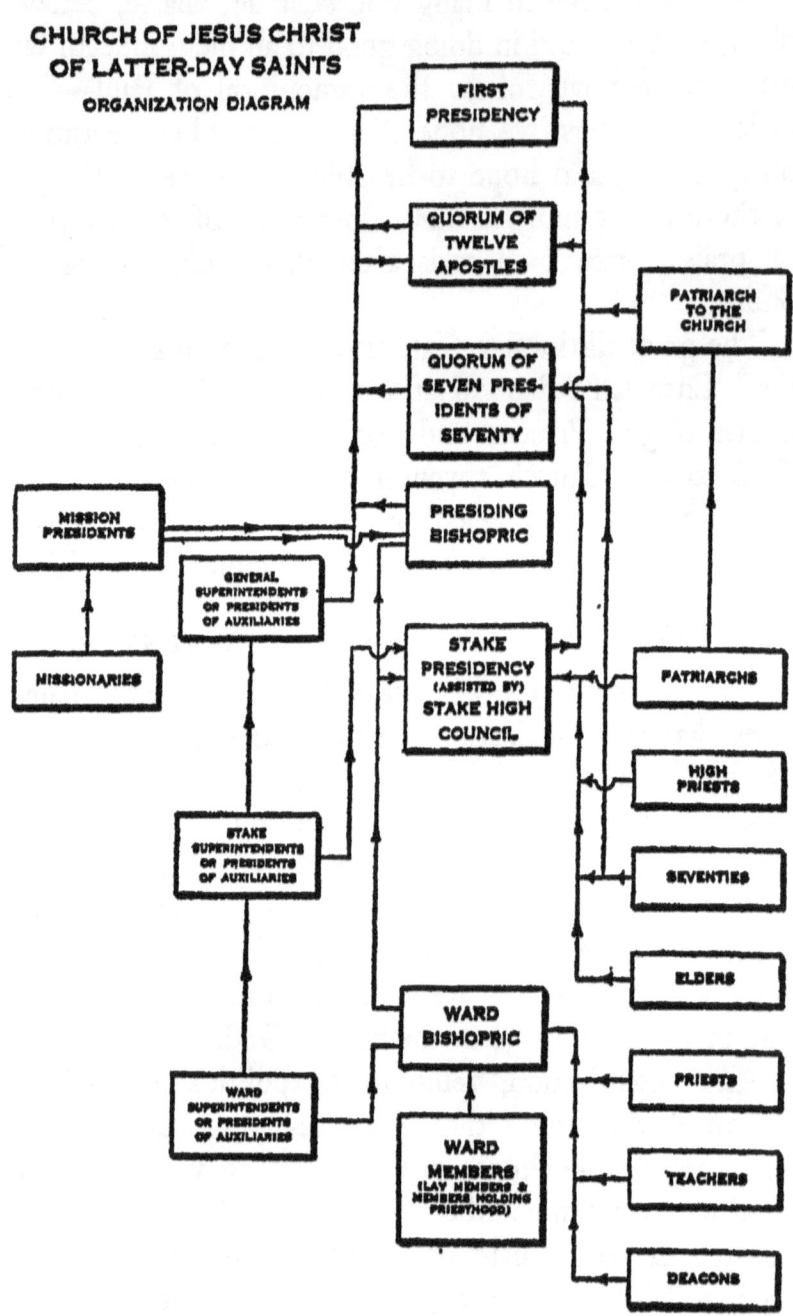

especially ordained to, and commissioned in, their respective offices and callings.

It is by virtue of and through the Holy Priesthood, or the God given authority, that the Church of Jesus Christ of Latter-day Saints was organized and all of the ordinances belonging to it are performed.

The term "Priesthood" as used by the Church of Jesus Christ of Latter-day Saints, has two meanings, (1) the power and authority given by God to act in His name, (2) the body of men collectively and individually upon whom any degree of this authority has been conferred.

The priesthood, with its powers and privileges, was conferred upon men in the present dispensation by messengers sent from heaven. Specially ordained and authorized agents can confer such rights as they may have upon others through the use of proper words and "the laying on of hands." Before this is done, however, in the organized branches of the Church, the vote of the quorum or ward, to which the person is to be ordained, is first obtained.

The priesthood, or authority is divided into two general divisions known as the "Melchizedek" and "Aaronic" priesthoods. These priesthoods might be thought of as the spiritual and temporal priesthoods, these terms being descriptive of their respective functions.

The Melchizedek Priesthood* is named after Melchizedek, the ancient High Priest and King of Salem. To this priesthood belongs the right of presidency in the

---

*Originally this was called the "Holy Priesthood after the order of the Son of God"; but to avoid the too frequent repetition of His name it was called the Melchizedek Priesthood.

church. Through its keys and power come a knowledge of the mysteries of God, and its functions are to administer in spiritual things.

The Aaronic or Lesser Priesthood is named after Aaron, the brother of Moses. The power and authority of this priesthood pertain to the outward or temporal ordinances of the Gospel.

The men holding, respectively, the Melchizedek and Aaronic priesthoods, are ordained to special offices or callings, each having their specific duties and responsibilities. Those holding the Melchizedek Priesthood are divided into groups known as high priests, patriarchs, apostles, seventies and elders. Those holding the Aaronic Priesthood are known respectively as priests, teachers, or deacons.

According to the revelations from God, certain of the Church and Priesthood officers must be ordained to specific offices in the priesthood. Thus, the President of the Church and his counselors, the presidents of high priest quorums, stake presidents, high councilors, and bishops must all hold the office of high priest in the Melchizedek Priesthood.

The chief or presiding council (quorum) of the Church is the First Presidency, which consists of three High Priests—a president and two counselors; its jurisdiction and authority are universal, extending over all the affairs of the Church in both temporal and spiritual things. The President of the Church is regarded as the mouthpiece of God to the Church, and he alone receives the law for the Church through revelation.

The second council (quorum) of the Church, standing next to the First Presidency, is composed of the Twelve Apostles. It is their duty, under the direction of the First Presidency, to supervise the work of the Church in all the world, to ordain evangelical ministers, and to act as special witnesses to the world of the divine mission of the Savior Jesus Christ.

The third council or quorum of the Church is the Seven Presidents of Seventy who labor under the direction of the Twelve Apostles. The seven presidents of this first quorum preside over all other quorums of seventies and their presidents.

The members of the above three councils are all bearers of the Melchizedek or higher Priesthood and have authority, when appointed, to officiate in all the ordinances of the Gospel under the direction of the First Presidency.

The presiding council (quorum) of the Aaronic or lower Priesthood is the Presiding Bishopric, consisting of the Presiding Bishop and two counselors, who have jurisdiction over all the offices of the Aaronic Priesthood in temporal affairs, under the direction of the First Presidency.

The General Authorities of the Church are presented frequently before the body of the Church throughout their ministry—to be sustained or rejected as leaders and presiding officers. The stake and ward officers are periodically subject to a similar regulation. Persons engaged constantly in Church service are supported, or partly sustained, according to need, from the Church funds. Missionaries have no stipends, they pay their own expenses or rely upon relatives or friends whom the Lord may raise up to their aid. There are on an average between two and three thousand missionaries devoting their full time to the labors of the ministry in the United States and foreign countries.

The missionary system of the church is unique. Both men and women members accept the call to do missionary work and render their services without remuneration. Full time missionaries thusly called and ordained serve for an average of two and one-half years, after which they return to their various private vocational occupations.

The revenue of the Church is derived from the tithes. One-tenth of a member's interest or increase each year is tithing. While this is a free-will offering, the law of the tithe applies to all members.

A Ward or Local Church

Consists of the following:

Bishopric (3 High Priests) a Bishop and two Counselors
Priesthood Quorums
Relief Society Presidency
Sunday School
Young Men's and Young Women's Mutual Improvement Association
Primary Association
Religion Class Association
Genealogical Society
Junior Seminary Classes

The ward is the local Church unit completely organized within itself, but responsible to and cooperating with the stake to which it belongs and the General Church authorities.

There are as many wards in each stake as necessary and as the Church grows in numbers, within the territory or organized stakes, more wards are organized.

Ward Bishopric

The office of bishop is the highest office of the lesser or Aaronic Priesthood. The Bishop with his two counselors, also high priests, form the ward bishopric. The bishop as high priest, presides over all councils, quorums and members holding the Melchizedek Priesthood within the ward.

The bishopric is responsible to the Stake Presidency, Stake High Council and Presiding Bishopric.

Ward Superintendents of Auxiliaries

There is no definite number. They are appointed as assistants to the bishopric in presiding over auxiliary organizations within the ward. They are responsible to the ward bishopric and stake superintendents.

Deacons

Twelve deacons form a quorum, one of the twelve is chosen president. The president is assisted by two counselors also chosen from the twelve and the three compose a presidency. The bishop of the ward presides over this presidency.

Deacons, as well as other officers of the Church, can

perform the duties of their office only under the direction of those who preside over them.

The office of deacon is an appendage to the lesser or Aaronic Priesthood and is the first office in that Priesthood. The deacons' duties are chiefly of a temporal nature in assisting in local matters. Deacons do not have authority to baptize, administer the sacrament, or lay on hands to confirm members to the Church or bestow the Holy Ghost. They are directly responsible to the ward bishopric.

Teachers

Twenty-four teachers form a quorum. One of this number is chosen as president and two are chosen counselors.

The teachers' duties are chiefly of a temporal nature, broader in scope, however, than those of deacon, and are directly responsible to the ward bishopric.

The office of teacher is an appendage to the lesser or Aaronic Priesthood and is the second office in the Priesthood.

Teachers do not have authority to baptize, administer the sacrament, lay on hands to confirm members to the Church or bestow the Holy Ghost.

Priests

Forty-eight priests form a quorum. The president of the quorum is the bishop of the ward. The priest's duties are more of a spiritual nature than either the deacon's or teacher's.

The priest has authority to baptize by immersion and to administer the sacrament. Priests do not have authority to confirm persons members of the Church who have been baptized, nor to lay on hands for the gift of the Holy Ghost.

The office of priest is the third and highest in the Aaronic Priesthood. The bishop of the ward is the presiding officer of the Aaronic Priesthood in his ward. The priests are directly responsible to the ward bishopric.

Elders

The office of elder is the first office in the higher or Melchizedek Priesthood. Ninety-six elders form a quorum out of which a president and two counselors are chosen.

The duties of an elder are chiefly of a spiritual nature, in conducting meetings, fulfilling missions, etc. The elder is the standing home minister.

The elders are responsible to the Stake Presidency and Stake High Council.

An elder has authority to ordain others to the office of elder and all other offices of the Priesthood.

Seventies

Each quorum of seventy is composed of seventy members holding the Melchizedek Priesthood. The seventies constitute the second office in the Melchizedek Priesthood. From among the seventy members a Council consisting of seven Presidents is chosen. The seventh president of the seven, counting from the one last ordained, presides over the six. When a vacancy occurs the one whose ordination is oldest in the Council of Seventy becomes the Senior President.

The chief duty of the seventy is to preach the doctrines of the Church both at home and abroad under the direction of the Twelve Apostles. Their calling is especially that of foreign ministry.

A seventy has authority to ordain others to the office of seventy and all other divisions of the Priesthood.

High Priests

The high priest is the third office in the Melchizedek Priesthood. There is no limit to the number in each quorum. In each quorum one high priest is chosen as president of the quorum and two high priests are chosen as his counselors.

There is generally only one quorum of high priests in each stake. The high priests' quorum is responsible to the Stake High Council and Stake Presidency.

The high priest has authority to ordain others to the office of high priest and all other divisions of the Priesthood.

The duties of a high priest are chiefly of a spiritual nature, in presiding over Church organizations.

Patriarchs

Patriarchs are evangelists and high priests, specially called and ordained to give blessings to the church members, within their stake or district. There is no definite number.

They are responsible to the Stake Presidency and to the Patriarch to the Church.

LATTER-DAY SAINTS

Stake High Council

Each stake (geographical area) has twelve high priests and six alternates which form the High Council of that stake and is presided over by the Stake Presidency. The High Council functions in a judicial manner assisting the Stake Presidency. It has appellate as well as original jurisdiction. Appeal from its decisions may be taken to the First Presidency.

It is directly responsible to the Stake Presidency.

The stake president presides as president of the Stake High Council.

Stake

A stake is a certain geographic division of the Church, comprising an indefinite number of wards. It has a distinct and definite organization which cooperates and supervises the wards within its boundaries.

In districts where the number of Church members is small or scattered, as in the mission field, the Stake Presidency is replaced by a mission president and the ward bishopric by a district or branch president, or by a presiding elder.

A Stake Presidency consists of a president and two counselors chosen by the president. All three are high priests.

The functioning of a Stake Presidency is confined to the particular stake over which it presides.

It is assisted by the Stake High Council, composed of twelve high priests.

It supervises all stake affairs and all wards within its boundaries.

Stake Superintendents of Auxiliaries

There is no definite number. They are appointed by the Stake Presidency as assistants to the Stake Presidency and High Council, to preside over the auxiliary organizations of the Stake.

They are responsible to the General Superintendents, Stake Presidency and Stake High Council.

Mission Presidents

In the unorganized stakes throughout the world the work of missionaries is carried on in "preaching the Gospel" and organizing branches, etc., under the direction of a mission president, who is ordained to preside over a designated area called a mission.

The various states of the United States where no organized stake exists, are thus organized into missions. Foreign countries are also organized and the work carried on under the direction of mission presidents.

The mission presidents are responsible to the Presiding Bishopric, Quorum of the Twelve Apostles and the First Presidency.

Patriarch to the Church

The appointment of the Patriarch to the Church is vested in the First Presidency.

His chief duty is to give blessings to the Church as a whole as well as its members individually.

He is a high priest and is responsible to the Quorum of the Twelve Apostles and the First Presidency.

LATTER-DAY SAINTS

The Presiding Bishopric

The appointment of the Presiding Bishop of the Church is vested solely in the First Presidency, who also has the sole power of removal. The Presiding Bishop chooses two counselors and together they form the Presiding Bishopric of the Church.

The Presiding Bishop presides over the lesser (Aaronic) Priesthood of the Church.

The Presiding Bishopric has charge of the Church property, and in connection with the First Presidency, handles the financial affairs of the Church.

The Presiding Bishopric is responsible to the Quorum of Twelve Apostles and the First Presidency.

They preside over all bishops in the Church.

General Superintendents of Auxiliaries

There is no definite number. Each General Superintendent has two counselors, the three forming a superintendency. The General Superintendencies preside over all auxiliary organizations of the Church. They are responsible to the Twelve Apostles and the First Presidency.

The Seven Presidents of Seventy

They are called the First Quorum of the Seventy, a quorum equal in authority to that of the Twelve Apostles. This quorum consists of seven ordained seventies. The seventh president of the seven, counting from the last one ordained, presides over the six and is designated as the Senior President.

Their duty is to organize Quorums of Seventy throughout the Church and to preach the gospel in all the world. They preside over all other Quorums of Seventy.

They act under the direction of the Twelve Apostles and are also responsible to the First Presidency.

Every decision made by either of these quorums (Twelve Apostles and Seven Presidents of Seventy) must be by the unanimous voice of the same; that is, every member in each quorum must be agreed to its decisions, in order to make their decisions of the same power or validity one with the other.

And in case that any decision of these quorums is made in unrighteousness, it may be brought before a general assembly of the several quorums, which constitute the spiritual authorities of the church; otherwise there can be no appeal from their decision.

The Quorum of The Twelve Apostles

Twelve men ordained to the Apostleship constitute the quorum of the Twelve Apostles, and there is but one such quorum in the Church. This quorum is equal in authority and power to the First Presidency.

This quorum has a president who is the senior member, that is, the one longest ordained.

It is customary for this quorum to sit in council with the First Presidency regarding the affairs of the Church.

They hold the authority to preside over the whole Church when there is no First Presidency.

They are responsible to the First Presidency only. The Apostles are, as the First Presidency, Prophets, Seers and Revelators to the Church.

Whenever a First Presidency needs to be organized, the Twelve Apostles may appoint and establish that quorum.

The Twelve Apostles are special witnesses of the name of Christ in all the world.

They may sit as a judicial body and try cases properly within their jurisdiction and from their unanimous decision there is no appeal.

They are chosen either by direct revelation from God, or by the First Presidency as directed by inspiration.

The First Presidency

The highest council or quorum in the Church is the First Presidency. In this body reside all the known powers of church government.

Three persons, who become the Presiding High Priests, constitute the First Presidency, namely the president and two counselors. The death of the President of the Church dissolves the First Presidency, and the quorum of the Twelve Apostles, under divine direction, nominate and ordain a President who chooses two counselors.

The President occupies the chief place, or first rank of all officers in the Church. He is the Presiding High Priest over the High Priesthood of the Church and is therefore at the head of all presidents, bishops, all councils and quorums, and all organizations and authorities in the whole Church in all the world.

The President is the Prophet, Seer and Revelator for the entire Church.

CHAPTER VIII

CONGREGATIONAL AND CHRISTIAN CHURCHES

Those adhering to the Congregational doctrines are located in the order of their numbers in the following places: North America, Europe, Asia, Africa, Islands, South America. Their total number is approximately 0.25% of the world's and 0.76% of the total Christian population.

Historical Sketch

The Reformation in England developed along three lines: Anglicanism, Puritanism and Separatism. The Anglicans held to the old English Church, minus the papacy and the distinctively papal features. The Puritans including the Presbyterians and some Anglicans, held to the National Church, believing that they should remain within the church and thus secure its reformation. The Separatists held that the whole system of the Establishment was an anti-Christian imitation of the true church and could not be reformed and that the only thing to do was to withdraw.

The development of the Separatists into Congregationalists began in 1604. Congregationalism is a type of church organization in which each individual congregation, or local church, has free control of all its own affairs. The principle upon which this plan was originally based is that each local congregation has as its head Jesus Christ alone, and that the relations of the several congregations are those of fellow-members in one common family of God. Thus Congregationalism eliminates such intermediary authorities as bishops and presbyteries. The movement to which the name was applied arose among those who held such views that they could not subscribe to the requirements of the Act of Uniformity (1559) or other government measures and so were unable to remain within the Established Church. Among these Separatists was Robert Browne, whose writings contain the first theoretical exposition of Congregational principles known. A church established on these lines was started in Southwark, London, in 1616; but not until the Protectorate did the Congregationalists make much progress. About that time the name Independents was first introduced. It was long used in Great Britain, but never found acceptance in America. In 1658, when the Savoy Synod met in London, 120 churches were represented. With the Restoration came repression for the Independents, relieved in 1689 by the Toleration Act. The most marked tendency among English Congregationalists in the 19th century was toward combination in larger fellowship. A union of the churches of the denomination in Scotland was formed in 1812, in Ireland in 1829; and in 1832 the Congregational Union of England and Wales was established. The Congregational Union and the Evangelical Union were united in 1896. Congregationalism was brought to America by the members of John Robinson's congregation (Robinson, however, remained in Holland), originally of Scrooby, England, when they landed from the Mayflower at Plymouth, in 1620. For some time Congregationalism in New England was practically a state religion. In 1648 in the Cambridge Platform a summary was drawn up to indicate the relations of the churches to one another and express the doctrinal views they held. There were then about 50 Congregational churches and few others in New England.

The withdrawal of the Massachusetts charter in 1684 replaced Congregationalism by Episcopacy, but a new charter in 1691 restored the former condition to a considerable degree. With the organization later of other denominations, Congregationalism gradually ceased to be the State religion. Before the close of the 18th century, delegates were interchanged between Presbyterian general assembly and several Congregational associations in the New England states.

The early part of the 19th century brought the Unitarian secession, when in all about 120 churches were separated from the main Congregational body. Out of state-wide "Conferences" developed national councils. The first regular National Council of the Congregational Churches of the United States met at Oberlin, Ohio, in 1871. Since then there have been meetings at stated intervals, first triennially, and later biennially. The National Council of 1913 adopted a platform which met with practically unanimous acceptance. But each local church is free to make its own declaration of faith and free to decide its own form of worship, and in the conduct of the local church, each member has an equal voice. In education Congregationalists have always been

CONGREGATIONAL AND CHRISTIAN 97

prominent, but the institutions they have founded—Harvard College (1636), Yale (1701), Williams, Amherst, Oberlin, and many others—have been free from sectarianism. The trend toward broader fellowship and larger cooperation was notably indicated in the merging of the National Council of the Congregational Churches of the United States and the General Convention of the Christian Church in 1931, held at Seattle, Washington, to form the General Council of the Congregational and Christian Churches.

At the present time, Congregationalists, Methodists and Presbyterians of Canada, are united in "The United Church of Canada," and the distinctive lines separating these three denominations have there been done away with. In the western part of America, many Congregational and Presbyterian bodies have consolidated under the name "Federated Church."

Doctrine

Congregationalism is a combination of two principles: (1) The independence of the local church, with complete control of all its concerns. (2) Fellowship of such independent churches in voluntary association. These principles exclude alike prelacy and presbyterianism, and make the local church supreme in matters of faith and practice.

As a result, while there is no authoritative Congregational creed—acceptance of which is a condition of ecclesiastical fellowship—there have been several statements of this consensus, culminating in a creedal statement which, while it has no formal ecclesiastical endorsement, is widely accepted as a fair statement of the doctrinal position of the Congregational churches.

The first of these statements, called the "Cambridge Platform," drawn up by a Synod summoned by the Massachusetts legislature, 1648, simply registered general approval of the Westminster Confession. Certain phraseology in that confession, however, proved unacceptable to many churches, and the Massachusetts revision, 1680, of the Savoy Confession and the Saybrook Platform of 1708, embodied the most necessary modifications, but still approved the general features of the Westminster Confession. The first National Council, in 1865, adopted the "Burial Hill Declaration," setting forth the right hand of fellowship to all believers "on the basis of those great fundamental truths in which all Christians should agree." But in the changing conditions this was not entirely satisfactory, and in 1880, the national council appointed a commission to prepare "a formula stating in precise terms the doctrines held today."

The commission composed of 25 representative men, finished its work in 1883. The statement, or creed, was never formally adopted, but was issued to the world "to carry such weight of authority as the character of the commission and the intrinsic merit of its exposition of truth might command." While there has been no official adoption of this creed by any general body—national council or state association—as binding upon the churches, yet it has furnished the doctrinal basis for a great many of the churches, and in the main has represented their general belief.

Thirty years later, in revising the constitution of the

National Council, a "Statement of Faith" was embodied in that instrument, which does not thereby become binding on the churches but which has been accepted by many of them as their creed, either with or without modification.

The Lord's Supper is free to all followers of Christ. Infant baptism is customary; although sprinkling is the mode commonly used, the form is optional.

Organization and Government

While the polity of the Congregational Churches is based upon certain definite principles, yet its elasticity may be observed by the following platform adopted by the National Council, "We believe in the freedom and responsibility of the individual soul and the right of private judgment. We hold to the autonomy of the local church and its independence of all ecclesiastical control. We cherish the fellowship of the churches united in district, State and national bodies, for counsel and co-operation in matters of common concern." In its historical development it represents adaptation to conditions rather than accord to a theory of church government.

The system is characterized by the absence of authority. Not even in the local church, will authority to act independently of the membership be delegated for a single year to a session or other official body. The local field is so limited and compact that the membership can administer its current affairs as a direct or pure democracy.

The larger fellowship bodies are so extensive that Congregationalism as a whole has perforce become a

100 HIS MANY MANSIONS

CONGREGATIONAL AND CHRISTIAN CHURCHES
ORGANIZATION DIAGRAM

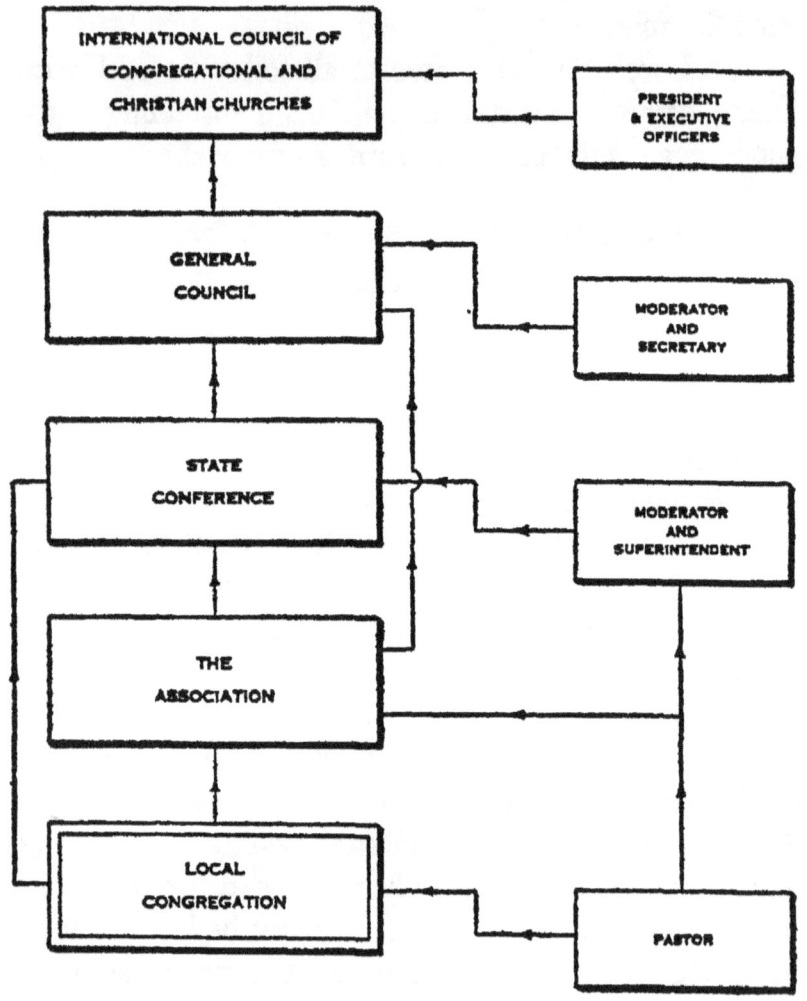

Note Arrows point in direction of cooperating bodies and officials in their relative positions. All assemblies or bodies above that of the local congregation are for advisory fellowship and service purposes only, having no jurisdiction in matters of doctrine or government

The double line around the local church indicates its independent or autonomous character.

representative democracy. But nowhere does the system admit authority of a higher body over a lower, a right to legislate, enforce measures or coerce to action. Each Congregational organization—local church, district association, state conference, national council—is free and sovereign in its own district sphere. All union of the lower bodies to form a higher, and all cooperation in the larger forms of work, are voluntary and unconstrained.

Admission to church membership is usually conditioned on the declared and evident purpose to lead the Christian life, rather than on the acceptance of any particular doctrine.

The local church is the unit and every church member, irrespective of sex or position, has an equal voice in its conduct and is equally subject to its control. For orderly worship and effective administration certain persons are set apart or ordained to particular services, but such ordination or appointment carries with it no ecclesiastical authority. In most churches there is a church committee which considers various topics relating to the conduct of the church, meets persons desiring to unite with it, and presents these matters in definite form for action by the church as a whole. Early in Congregational history there was a distinction between elders and deacons corresponding very closely to that in the Presbyterian Church. That distinction has disappeared, and the offices of elders, or spiritual guides, and of deacons, or persons having charge of the temporalities of the Church, have been united in the deaconate.

For fellowship and mutual assistance the churches gather in local associations or conferences, and in State conferences in which each church is represented by pastor and lay delegates. Membership in the National or General Council includes ministerial and lay delegates elected by the State conferences and the district associations. Membership in an association is generally regarded as essential to good and regular standing in the denomination, although any church may claim its right of independence and still be a Congregational church. No association or conference, or national council, however, has any ecclesiastical authority. That is vested solely in the council called by the local church for a specific case, and its existence terminates with the accomplishment of its immediate purpose. The result is that there is no appeal from one court to another, although an aggrieved party may call a new council, which, however, has no more authority than its predecessor.

Ordination to the ministry is generally by a council of churches called by the church of which the candidate is a member, or over which he is to be installed as a pastor. More and more, in practice, such councils are made up of the members of the district association of which the church is a constituent part. Doctrinal tests are less rigidly applied than in the past, practical Christian fellowship being emphasized rather than creed subscription. In the early history of Congregationalism the minister was a member of the church, selected by the church, and ordained to the service by a council of associate churches. However, his standing became recognized as having a permanent character, although the minister, whether pastor or not, still remained a member of his church, and subject to its order. For purposes of fellowship, ministerial associations have been formed, and in some cases these have furnished the basis of ministerial standing; but of late there has been a tendency to vest such standing in a church association or conference.

The Local Church

Consists of the following:

> Pastor
> Board of Deacons
> Board of Trustees
> Clerk
> Treasurer
> Auditor
> Church School Superintendent
> Church Committee
> Church School
> Young People's Society of Christian Endeavor
> Women's Missionary Society
> Men's Club

The pastor is the leader of the congregation and is responsible entirely to them. In a missionary church (not self-supporting), the pastor reports to the superintendent of the conference.

The local congregation is autonomous in matters of doctrine and church government.

The Association

Usually ten or more churches in a vicinity unite by appointing delegates, consisting of one pastor and a number of lay delegates from each church. The number of lay delegates depending upon the size of the church. It meets annually or semi-annually. It ordains ministers and acts for the mutual helpfulness and advice for its members.

In larger centers these associations may become incorporated executive bodies for the carrying on of missionary work, in addition to the rendering of other services to its member churches.

The State Conference

This is comprised of delegates from each church in the designated geographic area, on the basis of the pastor or pastors and lay delegates from each church. The number of lay delegates depending on the size of the congregation. It meets annually.

Where there is no Association, the State Conference ordains the ministers. Its purpose is in an advisory capacity and promotion of mutual interests.

It is an executive body in that it administers home missionary funds and maintains an organism for the service of the churches in general.

The General Council

This consists of delegates from the Associations, on the basis of one delegate from each Association, plus an additional delegate for each additional ten churches or major fraction thereof. Also two delegates from each State Conference, one of whom must be a woman, and two additional delegates from each 10,000 in addition to the first 10,000 members, half of whom must be women. The General Council constitutes a united body by the device which makes every member of the General Council a corporate member of every one of the missionary and educational societies, both home and foreign.

Delegates are divided as nearly equal as practicable between ministers and laymen.

The term of delegates is four years, one-half being elected at each biennial convention.

It meets every two years. Its purpose is to unify the work and to further cooperation among Congregational bodies throughout the country. It also elects committees and commissions, both temporary and permanent for general missionary, social service and inter-church relations.

(The General Convention of the Christian Church, as well as the National Council of Congregational Churches, maintains a skeleton organization for the purpose of conserving any legal interests which may appear in the future.)

The International Council of Congregational and Christian Churches

It consists of an unlimited number of delegates from any Congregational assembly. Meetings are held in different countries approximately every ten years. It acts as an international exchange of Congregational ideals, but has no jurisdiction over any Congregational body.

CHAPTER IX

DISCIPLES OF CHRIST

Those adhering to the Disciples' doctrines are located principally in the United States. Considerable numbers are to be found in England and Australia. Missionary work is carried on in many foreign countries.

HISTORICAL SKETCH

A Protestant religious body founded early in the 19th century in the United States. It originated in an effort to return to a form of Christianity with the Bible alone as basis for faith and conduct, apart from all the formulas and creeds. Thomas Campbell, a minister from the north of Ireland preaching in western Pennsylvania, came under the censure of his presbytery through his breadth of view in trying to gather into the Church scattered groups of Christians. He made a plea for unity among all Christians with no other platform than the primitive and simple gospel. He formed the Christian Association of Washington, Pennsylvania; but neither he nor his son Alexander, who joined him in the work, desired that it should develop into a new and distinct denomination. A church was established in 1811 and the movement expanded. Another minister, Barton W. Stone, with several associates, had also broken away from the Presbyterian Church and formed a church under the name of "Christians." Both Stone and Alexander Campbell had

DISCIPLES OF CHRIST

adopted immersion, and this brought them into sympathetic relations with the Baptists, but there was not enough agreement for a lasting connection. In 1832 a union took place at Lexington, Kentucky, between the followers of Stone, who wished to retain the name "Christians," and those of Campbell, who preferred to use "Disciples." The resulting church was known as the Christian Church, the Church of Christ and the Disciples' Church. After the Civil War the development was strong and rapid in the central and western States, particularly. There are considerable numbers of the Disciples in England and Australia, and missionary labors have been extended to the Far East, Africa, and other regions. A distinctive feature of the Church is the weekly celebration of the Lord's Supper. A separation into two parties has taken place during the 20th century, the progressive group being known as the Disciples of Christ, and the conservatives as Churches of Christ.

Doctrine

In addition to beliefs, in which they are in general accord with other Protestant churches, the Disciples hold certain positions which they regard as distinctive:

1. Feeling that "to believe and to do only those things enjoined by our Lord and His Apostles as being infallibly safe:" they aim "to restore in faith and spirit and practice the Christianity of Christ and His Apostles as found in the pages of the New Testament."

2. Affirming that "the sacred Scriptures as given of God answer all purposes of a rule of faith and practice,

and a law for the government of the church, and that human creeds and confessions of faith spring out of controversy and, instead of being bonds of union, tend to division and strife"—they reject all such creeds and confessions.

3. They place especial emphasis upon "the Divine Sonship of Jesus," as the fundamental fact of Holy Scripture, the essential creed of Christianity, and the one article of faith necessary to baptism and church membership.

4. Believing that in the Scriptures "a clear distinction is made between the law and the gospel," they "do not regard the Old and New Testament as of equally binding authority upon Christians," but hold that "the New Testament is as perfect a constitution for the worship, government, and discipline of the New Testament church as the Old was for the Old Testament church."

5. While claiming for themselves the New Testament names of "Christian," or "Disciples," "they do not deny that others are Christians or that other churches are Churches of Christ."

6. Accepting the divine personality of the Holy Spirit, through whose agency regeneration is begun, they hold that man "must hear, believe, repent, and obey the gospel" to be saved.

7. Repudiating any doctrine of "baptismal regeneration," and insisting that there is no other prerequisite to regeneration than confession of faith, with the whole heart in the personal living Christ, they regard baptism by immersion "as one of the items of the original divine

system," and as "commanded in order to the remission of sins."

8. Following the apostolic model, the Disciples celebrate the Lord's Supper on each Lord's Day "not as a sacrament, but as a memorial feast," from which no sincere follower of Christ of whatever creed or church connection is excluded.

9. The Lord's Day with the Disciples is not the Sabbath, but a New Testament Institution, consecrated by apostolic example.

10. The Church of Christ is a divine institution; sects are unscriptural and unapostolic, and the sect name, spirit, and life should give place to the union and co-operation that distinguishes the church of the New Testament.

Organization and Government

The government of the Disciples of Christ's Church is congregational in form. The officers of the church are the pastor, elders, and deacons. The elders have special care of the spiritual interests of the congregation, and the deacons of its financial affairs and benevolences, although this distinction between elders and deacons is not always observed. Applicants for the ministry are ordained by authority of the local church. The minister is a member of the church where he is located, whether as pastor or as evangelist, and is amenable to its discipline.

In accordance with the principles that have been emphasized in their history, the Disciples of Christ, individually, in their local church organization, in their

110 HIS MANY MANSIONS

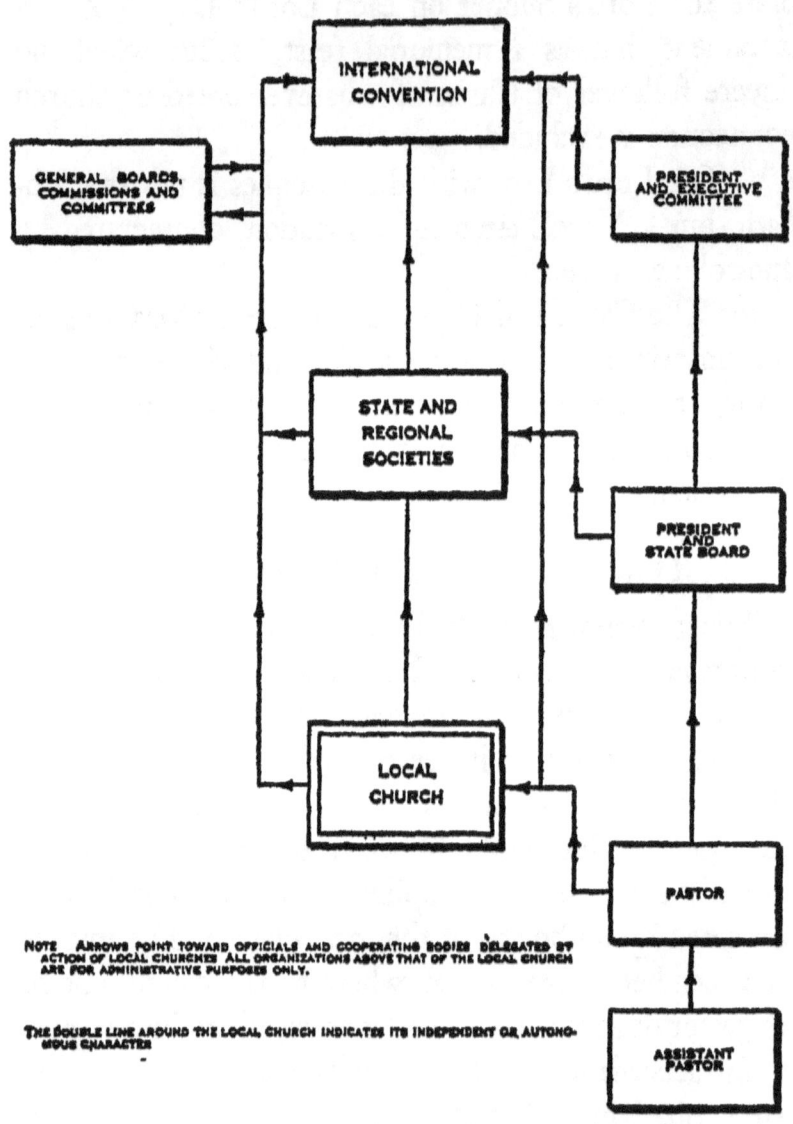

organized societies, and in their denominational relations, have constantly sought to overcome denominational distinction, and to secure the unity of the church in its broadest sense.

There is an "International Convention of Disciples of Christ," composed of individual members of the churches. The convention as such has no authority over the action of the churches, which are at liberty to accept or reject its recommendations.

There is no national ecclesiastical organization of the churches. For conference in regard to ministerial matters, and a general supervision over ministerial standing, ministerial associations are formed, but they are simply advisory, the authority resting with the local church of which the minister is a member.

The Local Church

Consists of the following:

> Pastor
> Board of Elders
> Board of Deacons
> Deaconesses
> Board of Trustees
> Clerk
> Treasurer
> Auditor
> Superintendent of Church School
> Young People's Society
> Women's Organization
> Men's Organization

The local church is autonomous in matters of doctrine

and church government. Each, however, holds to the general form and trend of the other organizations of the church as a whole.

The pastor or minister is the leader in the local congregation and the other officers act as his staff in carrying out the working of the local affairs.

Each local church may choose one delegate for each 100 members or fraction thereof (limit 5) to attend the International Convention which meets each year. This is purely optional on the part of the church.

State Society

It conducts the work in the state by cooperating with the local churches, and acts as a cooperating body with the various national boards and the local churches. It establishes new local churches where needed.

Its officers and directors are chosen from among the local churches.

Regional Society

In states of fewer memberships such as Idaho and Washington, the Missionary Society may be combined into what is known as the "Regional Society." There are only four of these in the United States. Their organization is similar to that of the State Society.

International Convention

Its organization consists of a president, three vice-presidents, general secretary, recording secretary, transportation secretary, treasurer and an executive committee consisting of fifteen additional persons. The officers and

DISCIPLES OF CHRIST

the executive committee are the convention ad interim. There are also certain commissions appointed by the convention through which it functions ad interim.

Each local church may choose one delegate for each 100 members or fraction thereof. No church is permitted more than five delegates.

The convention meets annually and is composed of delegates from all the local churches who desire to send representatives. Any member of the church who attends is accorded the privilege of the convention.

This convention acts only in an advisory capacity. Reports are made to it, however, by the various boards and committees and actions are taken by it which are accepted by the boards as determining their policies.

General Boards, Commissions and Committees

The general boards are composed of the following:

>United Christian Missionary Society
>Board of Education
>Board of Temperance and Social Welfare
>Board of Pension Fund
>Board of Christian Unity
>State Secretaries Association

Each board and committee conducts its designated work in cooperation with all the churches. Churches contribute directly to the support of the various boards.

Each board is incorporated and as a legal entity chooses its own officers and directors.

Each board reports to the International Convention which acts in an advisory capacity to the various boards and committees.

CHAPTER X

EASTERN ORTHODOX CHURCHES
(Catholic)

Those adhering to the Eastern Orthodox Catholic doctrines are located, in the order of their numbers, in the following places: Europe, Asia, Africa, North America, (none recorded for South America nor the Islands). Their total number is approximately 6.9% of the world's and 18.1% of the total Christian population.

HISTORICAL SKETCH

The Eastern Orthodox churches compose the group of Christian churches of eastern Europe and western Asia, which recognize as the heads of the Church the patriarchs of Constantinople, Alexandria, Antioch, and Jerusalem. The term Orthodox is used of these Christians as the term Catholic is of other Christians of the West. The prime, fundamental difference between Catholics and Orthodox and the one on which all efforts of reunion have failed is the primacy of the pope as ruler of the Church; Orthodox allow him only a primacy of honor. The Orthodox churches are of the Byzantine rite; this rite also has many belonging to it who recognize the supremacy of the pope. The priests are married, the bishops are not. This has given rise to a deep distinction between the regular clergy (who are unmarried) and the seculars, for the rulers of the church, the bishops, are not drawn from the numbers of those who work in the parishes. In Russia particularly this caused continual friction and tended to make parishes hereditary in a family of priests and to remove the bishop from any connection with the people. The churches are generally square with a solid screen covered with icons separating the sanctuary from the rest of the church; Byzantine architecture was developed by Orthodox churches.

From the time of the Emperor Justinian the control throughout the East has been in the hands of the state, and the nationalism of the 19th century had very grave effects on the Church's constitution. There are at present some 17 autonomous Orthodox churches.

The Patriarchate of Constantinople, having a pre-eminence of honor in the East, was established when Constantinople was made the imperial capital; this was originally the patriarchate of Asia Minor and of Europe as far west as, and including, Serbia. From the time of Justinian the emperor had a firm hold over the election of the patriarch and controlled him absolutely. Under the Turkish empire he was much freer, except that the sultan exercised the investiture after his election and supervised his acts. The Moslem theocracy granted him many civil rights over Christians, and he was held responsible for the behavior of the Orthodox in the State as in the Church. Under the republic the patriarch of Constantinople is still the acknowledged head of the Orthodox of Turkey. As the countries of eastern Europe won their independence the patriarch lost his hold over them because of his intimate connection with the Turkish state.

The Patriarchate of Alexandria is now made up of the

few Greeks of northern Egypt; the Copts withdrew from the Orthodox communion before the Turkish invasion and they hold the original succession of patriarchs of Alexandria; the Orthodox patriarchate was established to replace the Monophysite patriarch.

The Patriarchate of Antioch was the ancient region of Syria and Near Eastern Asia (except Asia Minor); the Orthodox of Cilicia, Syria, and Iraq alone now recognize the authority of the Orthodox patriarch of Antioch.

The Patriarchate of Jerusalem was founded by the Council of Chalcedon to honor the Holy City; only a few Palestinian Greeks recognize the Orthodox patriarch of Jerusalem, who has charge of the holy places.

The Russian Orthodox Church, until the advent of the Soviet regime the greatest single Orthodox Church, was headed first by the metropolitan of Kiev, under Constantinople. The metropolitan see was moved to Moscow in the 14th century and given patriarchal dignity by the Patriarch of Constantinople in 1582. This fifth patriarchate remained such in theory after the office of patriarch was abolished (1721) by Peter the Great, who set up a Holy Synod instead. The Holy Synod, made up of bishops, was controlled by a layman (procurator), appointed by the tsar; by this change the tsar was made the constitutional ruler of the Russian Church. In 1917 the Holy Synod was replaced by a patriarch, but the vicissitudes of revolution have completely wrecked the organization, and the status of the Orthodox Church in Russia is now unknown.

The Orthodox Church of North America was organized independently after the foundation of the USSR.

EASTERN ORTHODOX

It has several bishoprics, but its constitution is uncertain because of the situation of the Orthodox immigrants, since the Greeks, the Syrians, and the Russians all have their own autonomous bishops.

The Orthodox Church of Georgia is really a very ancient church, using Georgian as its liturgical language; it became part of the Russian Church, and was separated again after the establishment of the USSR. The Orthodox Church of Estonia was organized after the World War; it is Estonian in liturgical language, but it derives its orders from Russia. The Orthodox Church of Finland is ruled by the archbishop of Helsingfors, and was separated from the Russian Church after the establishment of the USSR; The Orthodox Church of Poland is a similar foundation; it is made up largely of Russians in Poland. The Church of Cyprus has been independent since the Council of Ephesus, when it broke away from the Patriarchate of Antioch; it is Greek in language. The Church of Mt. Sinai is made up of the monastery of St. Catherine on Mt. Sinai and a few subject houses; its archbishop is appointed by the patriarch of Jerusalem. The Orthodox Church of Greece, established by law, made itself independent of Constantinople after the Greek War of Independence. It is governed by a Holy Synod. The Orthodox Church of Bulgaria was severed from communion by the four ancient patriarchates late in the 19th century, but the Russian Church recognized it. The Orthodox Church of Rumania is similar to that of Greece, except that Rumanian is its liturgical language. The Orthodox Church of the Serbs, Croats, and Slovenes is the state church of the Yugoslav monarchy, but it is almost entirely made up of Serbs. The Orthodox Church of Albania is not well organized and dates from the independence of the country. The history of the Orthodox Church is not marked by any great events since the schism of Photius, which really severed East and West, and the ex-communication of 1054 when the papacy (Rome) and the Patriarchate of Constantinople denounced each other. Twice there have been reunions with Rome; at the councils of Lyons and Florence (Basel and Ferrara-Florence). Both of these were unreal. The use of the clause Filioque in the Creed is regarded by many Orthodox as a great factor in the continued separation of the East from Rome. The Church of England has very cordial relations with some Orthodox, but there is no certain intercommunion between them.

Doctrine

The Liturgy is not usually celebrated daily as in the West, and it is always sung (i.e., there is nothing corresponding to low Mass). The sacraments differ from those of the West only in their ritual and in some features, e.g., priests may confirm; unction is administered to the sick whether in extremis or not; confession is much less common than in the West; communion in both kinds is given to the laity; infants receive communion. In general it may be said of the Orthodox that they have produced no organized systems of theological or legal thought. For this reason generalizations on the details of custom and dogma are difficult to make. Thus, the teaching on Purgatory is nebulous, and the conception of the Virgin is considered by some to have been immaculate.

EASTERN ORTHODOX

The Orthodox accept the first seven ecumenical councils and place very great emphasis upon them, generally holding that no dogmatic pronouncement may ever be made until another council meets. They are strenuously conservative of old customs and forms. The Holy Scriptures are interpreted strictly in accordance with the teachings of the seven ecumenical councils and the holy fathers. The Niceoconstantinopolitan Creed is held only in its original authoritative form, without the Roman-Latin addition of the "Filioque" phrase. Recognizing Christ as the only head of the earthly as well as of the heavenly church, they do not accept the dogma of the pope as the special representative or vicar of Christ on earth, and the infallible head of His earthly church.

According to their teachings, infallibility belongs to the whole assembly of true believers, to the "Ecclesia," or Church, which is represented by its council legally called together and whose decisions are confirmed by the consensus of the church.

They believe in the procession of the Holy Ghost from the Father alone; honor Mary as the mother of God, and honor the nine orders of angels and the saints; do not define as dogma the doctrine of the immaculate conception of the Virgin Mary (however, some do). They reject the doctrine of the surplus merits of the saints and the doctrine of indulgences.

They reverence relics of the saints, pictures of holy subjects, and the cross, but forbid the use of carved images. They accept seven sacraments—baptism, anointing (confirmation or chrismation), communion, penance, holy orders, marriage, and holy unction. Baptism of either infants or adults by threefold immersion (once each for the Father, the Son and the Holy Ghost) is recognized as the only proper form, although other forms are accepted of necessity or in the case of converts who have previously been baptized.

The sacrament of anointing with "chrism," or holy oil, is administered immediately after that of baptism and the christmated infant or adult is thereafter a full communicant in the Eucharist.

The doctrine of transubstantiation is accepted. In the Eucharist, leavened bread is used, being soaked in wine and offered, after confession and absolution, to all members of the Eastern Orthodox Churches. Children under seven years of age, however, receive the sacrament without confession. Holy unction is administered to the sick, and not alone to those in danger of death. The church rejects the doctrine of purgatory, but believes in the beneficial effect of prayer for the dead by the living and for the living by the dead. It rejects the doctrine of predestination, and considers that for justification both faith and works are necessary.

Divisions

The following churches, although they are distinct and independent bodies, have doctrines and church government substantially the same as those of the general Orthodox (Catholic) Churches.

Albanian Orthodox, Bulgarian Orthodox, Greek Orthodox, Greek Orthodox (Hellenic), Rumanian Orthodox, Russian Orthodox, Serbian Orthodox, Syrian Holy Orthodox, Orthodox Church of Poland, Orthodox

EASTERN ORTHODOX

Church of Finland, Orthodox Church of North America, Georgian Orthodox Church, Orthodox Church of Jerusalem.

Organization and Government

In the Eastern Orthodox Churches there are three orders of the ministry—deacons, priests, and bishops. The deacons assist in the work of the parish and in the service of the sacraments. Priests and deacons are of two orders, secular and monastic. Marriage is allowed to candidates for the deaconate and the priesthood, but is forbidden after ordination. The episcopate is, as a rule, confined to members of the monastic order. A married priest, should his wife die, may enter a monastery and take the monastic vows, and is eligible to the episcopate. The parishes are, as a rule, in the care of the secular priests. The highest office a married man can obtain in the ecclesiastical order is that of a priest.

The service of the Eastern Orthodox Churches is solemn and elaborate. It is essentially that of the earlier centuries of Christianity, and is most fully and completely observed in the monasteries.

There are no sculptured images and no instrumental music, although there are pictorial representations of Christ, the apostles and saints, and scenes in Bible history.

The most important service is the divine liturgy, the chief part of which is the celebration of the Eucharist. There are three liturgies, those of St. John Chrysostom, St. Basil the Great, and St. Gregory, the last called the liturgy of the "Presanctified Gifts," for which the holy gifts or emblems are prepared at a preceding service,

HIS MANY MANSIONS

EASTERN ORTHODOX CHURCHES

ORGANIZATION DIAGRAM

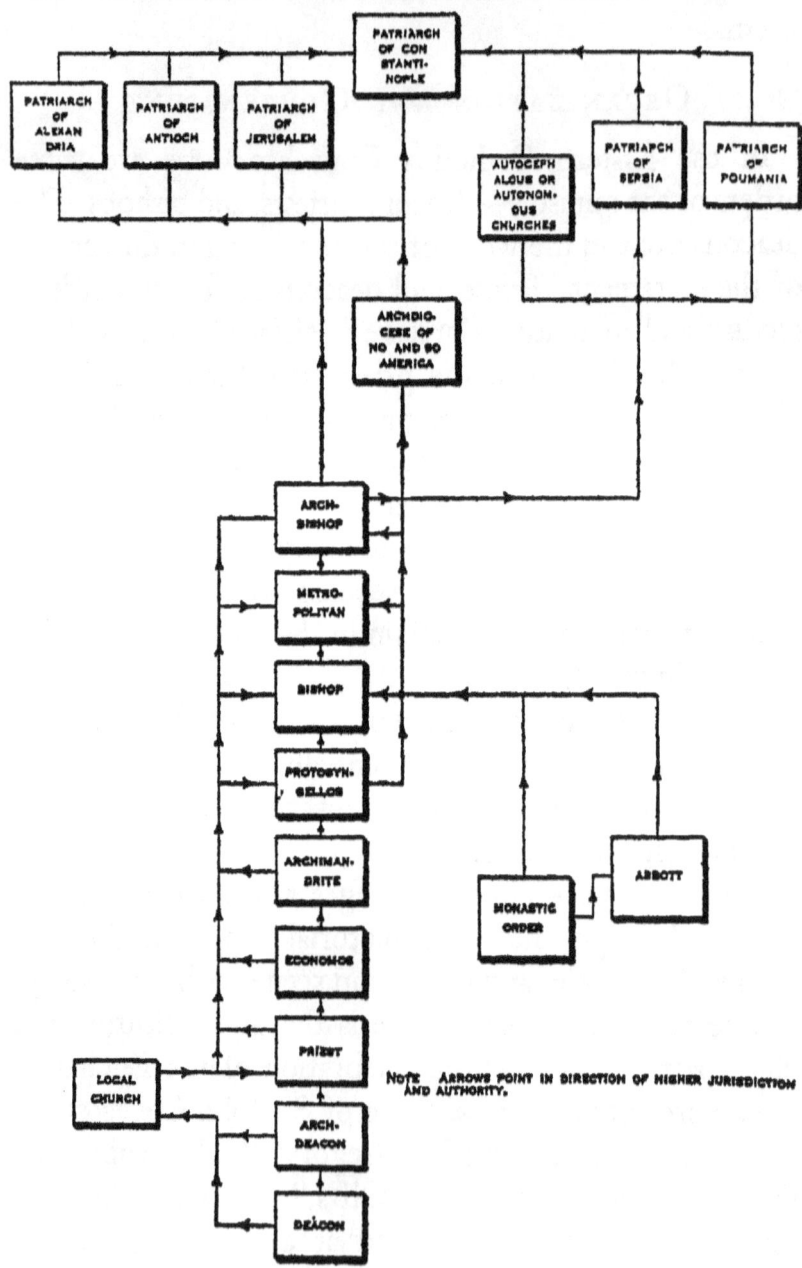

Note: Arrows point in direction of higher jurisdiction and authority.

generally that of St. Basil. There are no so-called "silent liturgies," or "private Masses," and two liturgies are not allowed to be performed in the same church simultaneously, nor can a liturgy be performed by the same priest, or on the same altar twice a day. A "corporal," otherwise known as "antimins"—a cloth with a particle of the holy remains of some saint sewn into it, and especially blessed by a bishop for every church—is necessary to the performance of the liturgy. Moreover, a priest may perform it only when he is fasting. Besides the liturgy, the church has vespers, vigils, matins, hours, and special prayers for various occasions and needs. The several services named consist of reading from the Old and New Testaments, supplicatory prayers, thanksgiving, glorifying, hymns, etc.

In countries where the Eastern Orthodox Church (Greek Orthodox) is the church of state, such as Greece, Rumania, etc., the offices of patriarch and archbishop are filled by choosing from a list of eligible officers, who are first approved by the state government, and then one is selected for either office and voted upon by the synod.

Above the office of Economos all or any officer is eligible to be chosen for any other higher office.

The organization for the general government of the different Eastern Orthodox Churches varies in different countries. In general, there is a council at the head of which, as president, is a bishop elected by the ecclesiastical representatives of the people. Historically, and at present in some cases, this presiding bishop is called the Patriarch, and has special colleagues and officers for the purpose of governing his flock. The largest or most important of the bishoprics connected with the patriarchate, or synod, are called "metropolitan sees," though the title now carries with it no special ecclesiastical authority. In early times, both the clergy and the laity of the local churches had a voice in the election of bishops, priests, and deacons, but of late that right has been much restricted, and at present the priests and deacons are usually appointed by the bishops, and the bishops are elected by the clergy.

Monks and nuns are gathered in monastic establishments or are scattered out in missionary work. In some monastic colonies the members live in communities, while in others they lead a secluded, hermetical life, each in his own cell. There is but one order, and the vows for all are the same, obedience, chastity, prayer, fasting and poverty. Each monastery is presided over by an abbot who is a priest generally of the rank of Archimandrite.

The Local Church

Consists of the following:

>Priests
>Deacons
>Board of Trustees
>Sunday School
>Educational Committee
>Societies

All spiritual matters are left strictly with the priest who may be one of the four following ranks: Protosyngellos, archimandrite, economos or priest. The priest is responsible to the Board of Trustees in any temporal matters.

EASTERN ORTHODOX

The Board of Trustees can dismiss and call the priest, subject to the approval of the archbishop, and has full control over all local church matters and property. A local congregation, consisting of members in full standing, elects the Board of Trustees. The Board of Trustees elects its own president and officers. There is generally one trustee elected for each fifty members voting.

In countries where the Orthodox religion is a religion of the state, it is taught daily in the public schools in addition to the church ceremonies.

Deacon

The deacon is the servant of the church. He assists the priests and other superior clergy in the performance of their duties, especially during the liturgy. He cannot baptize or take confessions. He is responsible in all temporal matters to the Board of Trustees of the church where he is serving. A married man can fill this office but he cannot become an officer of higher rank as long as he remains married.

Archdeacon

Archdeacon is the first ranking office of the deacon and is limited in his official capacity similar to that of the deacon.

Priest

A priest is the lowest ranking office in the four ranks of the priest office. He has authority to officiate in all general ecclesiastical matters of the church, including baptizing, dedicating and consecrating. A married man can advance no farther than this office.

Economos

This is the third office of priest and the duties of this office are the same as those of the priest. This being merely a priest office of higher rank.

Archimandrite

This is the second ranking office of priest and was originally the designated head of many monasteries. It corresponds to the office of father-provincial of the Roman Catholic Church.

Protosyngellos

He is a superior ranking priest and next to the bishop in the Deaconate of the Church. This office is almost in disuse at the present time. It may be found in the patriarchates and it corresponds to the office of the secretary to the metropolitan or archbishop.

Bishop

There are three offices of bishop, namely, bishop, metropolitan and archbishop. A bishop or "episcopos" is the chief prelate over the ecclesiastical affairs of the diocese (geographic division). He may be an assistant to an archbishop or metropolitan and ranks third in grade in clerical orders. The bishops meeting together and acting as a body are considered infallible in matters of doctrine, providing they represent the conscience of the church.

Metropolitan

A metropolitan is a particular office or rank of bishop. It is an ancient title conferred upon the bishop of a

EASTERN ORTHODOX

metropolis or capital city of a province. He may also be the bishop of a diocese. He is a superior ranking bishop.

Archbishop

This is the highest office next to the patriarch. He is the head of the Holy Synod of a national state church where there is no patriarch, or the head of a privileged province like the Americas.

Ecclesiastically the office of archbishop is equal to the office of patriarch, but in matters of administration the patriarch ranks higher. Every patriarch is an archbishop, but every archbishop is not a patriarch.

In America where there is no patriarch, the archbishop is supreme authority over all ecclesiastical matters.

Archdiocese of North and South America

The Archdiocese of North and South America is an ecclesiastical creation of the ecumenical Patriarchate of Constantinople. Its jurisdiction and influence extend over the entire Western Hemisphere, namely, North America, including Canada, and South America.

The affairs of the Church are conducted by a synod which is composed of the Archbishop of North and South America, the assistant Bishop, the Protosyngellos and the Archimandrite. These officers when acting in unison form the synod (ecclesiastical court) whose decisions are subject to the approval of the Patriarch of Constantinople.

The archbishop of North and South America is directly responsible in all spiritual matters to the Patriarch of Constantinople. There is no appeal however, from decisions of the Archbishop in spiritual or temporal matters.

Churches of the Various Countries Where Eastern Orthodox Catholicism is the State Church (Autocephalous or National Autonomous Churches).

The Ecumenical Patriarch as well as the other patriarchates and the independent state churches function through their "synods" composed of bishops over whom preside the patriarch in the patriarchates and the archbishop in the independent state churches.

The following are the autocephalous or autonomous Churches: Orthodox Church of Russia, Orthodox Church of Cyprus, Orthodox Church of Greece, Orthodox Church of Georgia, Orthodox Church of Iberia, Orthodox Church of Mt. Sinai, Orthodox Church of Poland, Orthodox Church of Finland, Orthodox Church of Esthonia, Orthodox Church of Czechoslovakia, Orthodox Church of Lettonia, Orthodox Church of Lithuania.

These autonomous or independent churches function through their Holy Synods and are presided over by the archbishops.

Each of the above listed churches has an organization composed of officers in rank as follows: Office of bishop—archbishop, metropolitan, bishop; office of priest—protosyngellos, archimandrite, economos, priest; office of deacon—archdeacon, deacon.

An autocephalous church is not under the spiritual authority of a patriarchate, while the autonomous churches are subject to certain limitations, and are more or less under the spiritual authority of a patriarchate. All, however, recognize the Patriarch of Constantinople as the supreme spiritual authority. He is called the Ecumenical Patriarch, and his office or seat is called the Ecumenical Patriarchate.

Patriarchates

All the patriarchates are independent and manage their affairs with complete independence. However, in matters of faith and order the Ecumenical Patriarch of Constantinople is recognized as the supreme authority for the entire Eastern Orthodox Church.

All patriarchates function through their Holy Synods, presided over by the patriarch.

A patriarchate is the jurisdiction or office of a patriarch, the patriarch being superior to the archbishop in the clerical order.

The Patriarchates of Constantinople, Alexandria, Antioch and Jerusalem are the original and established seats of the Eastern Orthodox Church. Two other jurisdictions are now recognized as patriarchates to some extent, these are Serbia and Rumania.

The jurisdiction of each patriarchate is as follows: (1) Ecumenical Patriarchate of Constantinople; over parts of Turkey and Greece. (2) Patriarchate of Alexandria; over the entire Africa. (3) Patriarchate of Antioch; over Syria. (4) Patriarchate of Jerusalem; over Palestine and Mount Sinai. (5) Patriarchate of Serbia; over the entire Kingdom of Jugoslavia. (6) Patriarchate of Rumania; over the entire Kingdom of Roumania.

CHAPTER XI

EPISCOPAL CHURCH OF ENGLAND

Those adhering to the Episcopalian doctrines are located, in the order of their numbers, in the following places: Europe, North America, Islands, Africa, Asia, South America. Their total number is approximately 1.2% of the world's and 3.2% of the total Christian population.

HISTORICAL SKETCH

The Church of England had its beginning as a separate national institution in the 16th century, when Henry VIII, withdrawing allegiance from the pope, announced that in England the king should be head of the church. The occasion of the break with Rome was Henry's request for divorce from Katherine of Aragon. The Act of Supremacy, 1534, acknowledged the king as "the only supreme head on earth of the Church of England." Thus the Reformation in England under Henry and Wolsey was at first a matter of policy, not doctrine. The theology of the Church as shown in the Six Articles (1539) and the King's book (1543) was unchanged in essentials. The monasteries were suppressed, chiefly at the hands of Thomas Cromwell. Henry authorized the Great Bible, a revision of the English translations of Tyndale and Coverdale, and some slight alterations in services.

The divorce of Henry VIII was not the sole cause leading up to the occasion of the break between England and Rome. If it had never happened, some other incident probably would have created the breach sooner or later. The king, in spite of his power, would not have accomplished the "break" had the country not been in a great measure hostile to the administrative policy of Rome. The question at the time was more jurisdictional than doctrinal.

Under Edward VI changes came rapidly and Protestantism gained ground. In 1549 the first Book of Common Prayer was adopted. Under Queen Mary all the measures that had separated the Church of England from Rome were reversed, legislation was repealed, the old ritual was brought back, and the nation was received again into the Catholic communion under the pope. Queen Elizabeth restored Protestantism. The national Church retained its continuity with the early Christian Church of Britain. It retained much of the ritualism sanctioned by older rubrics. In the struggle between Catholicism and Calvinism, the queen and her advisers hit upon a middle course. The Act of Supremacy made clear the constitutional position of the Church in relation to the crown. Provision was made that the powers thus restored to the sovereign should be exercised by a Court of High Commission. Throughout Elizabeth's reign, as the defender of Protestantism she was at war with the Catholic powers of Europe. Under James I the steadily rising tide of Puritanism made necessary the Hampton

Court Conference (1604), where the king gave his decision for the existing doctrine. Under Charles I the extreme measures of the party headed by Archbishop Laud, in maintaining the discipline and worship of the Church against the Calvinists, had much to do with bringing on civil war (1642). The Long Parliament, after excluding the bishops, substituted Presbyterianism for the Episcopacy in 1646, in accordance with the Solemn League and Covenant. Laud and the king were executed. Under Oliver Cromwell, Independent rather than Presbyterian doctrines triumphed; it was a penal offence to use the prayer book. Many bishops were imprisoned and many churches were pillaged. With the Restoration in 1660 the episcopacy was restored. The prayer book was in 1662 made the only legal service book by an Act of Uniformity which required the episcopal ordination of all ministers. About 2,000 clergymen, the "nonjurors," instead of complying, resigned and, with their adherents, established their own worship in Protestant nonconformist chapels. Parliament passed severe acts against nonconformists, 1661-73. In 1688 a petition to King James II against his order to read in all the churches a declaration of indulgence was signed by Sancroft, archbishop of Canterbury, and six other bishops. Imprisoned, they were on trial acquitted. Some of these were among the nonjurors who refused to swear allegiance to William and Mary. For some time Whigs and latitudinarians held control in the Church. The Church was in the period (1717-1852) without any "organ of corporate self-expression." There was a revival of religious fervor in the late 18th century one of the results of which was the

EPISCOPAL, CHURCH OF ENGLAND

rise of Methodism. In the first half of the 19th century certain Catholic elements in the Church of England were revived by the Oxford Movement, of which Keble and Pusey were leaders, and also Newman until he went over to the Church of Rome, 1845. To the later leaders of the movement, ritualism became of chief importance, as it is at present to the High Church party, which holds the doctrines of Apostolic succession, the Real Presence, and others that are contravened by the Low Church of Evangelical party. The Broad Church adherents follow a middle course. Meanwhile, ecclesiastical matters, both of doctrine and ritual, were settled by secular statesmen. From 1833 this jurisdiction belonged to the judicial committee of the privy council. Judgments were made in noted cases concerning baptismal regeneration and the nature of the Eucharist.

Worship of the Church of England is liturgical, and is regulated by the Book of Common Prayer. The creeds in use are the Apostles', the Nicene, and the Athanasian. The standards of doctrine are found in the Thirty-nine Articles, the Book of Common Prayer, the Catechism, and two Books of Homilies. In the Articles the truths of Christianity are explained on the authority of Scripture alone. Doctrines accepted universally are that of ~~~~~~; that of original sin; and that of ~~~~~~, God's purpose of redemption for "those whom he hath chosen in Christ out of mankind."

As the British Empire grew into a world empire, Anglicanism spread over all parts of the world. Yet it has no uniform organization. The real Church of England is limited to the dioceses of Canterbury and York.

Besides these, there are nine churches which administer their own affairs independently, but together with the mother church they form the Anglican Communion. They are as follows: The Church in Wales, in Ireland, the Episcopal Church in Scotland, the Protestant Episcopal Church in America, the Church in India, in Canada, in Australia and Tasmania, in South Africa and the Church in New Zealand. In all essential features, they agree with one another. But there are deviations in the government as well as in the liturgy, and even in the creed. The laity has a greater part in the administration of the church in the foreign polities (church governments). These churches have their own prayer books, with their deviations. The attitude to the ancient church creeds is not uniform.

The Episcopal Church—or the Protestant Episcopal Church in the United States of America—is the literal descendant of the Church of England, and dates, as a separate American ecclesiastical body, from 1789. The general position of the Episcopal Church is declared in the Preface to the Prayer Book, which states that "this church is far from intending to depart from the Church of England in any essential point of doctrine, discipline, or worship."

The earliest known services of the Church of England in the American colonies were conducted by the chaplains carried with the fleets of Frobisher in 1578, in New England; and Drake, in 1579, on a headland over-looking the present Bay of San Francisco. But not until 1607, was that church permanently established, when the Rev.

EPISCOPAL, CHURCH OF ENGLAND 135

Robert Hunt celebrated the Holy Communion on May 21, on the banks of the James River, Virginia.

The churches in the colonies were under the jurisdiction of the Bishop of London.

In New England, isolated attempts at church organization were made, but for many years none proved permanent, since the Puritans applied to the Anglicans the same proscription from which they themselves had fled.

The first English Church was opened in Philadelphia in 1685. In 1697, the charter for Trinity church was granted by the Royal Governor. Dean Berkeley, later Bishop of Cloyne, came to Newport, R. I., with the intention of founding a college. Although this project failed, he was one of the earliest supporters of Yale College and, on his return to Great Britain, had much to do with securing the charters for King's College, now Columbia University, New York, and for the Academy and College of Philadelphia, now the University of Pennsylvania.

The Church in America, prior to the revolution, was seriously handicapped by the lack of a bishop. Candidates for ordination were obliged to take the long and dangerous journey to England and the Bishop of London was unable to exercise the discipline, both of clergy and laity, which was at times greatly needed. Repeated appeals were made for the consecration of a bishop for the Colonies; but the plan was blocked, partly through political considerations and partly by reasons of the Puritan fear of an established church.

During the War of the Revolution, many of the churches were closed, and the loyalist clergy fled to England and Canada. On the other hand, some of the clergy steadfastly adhered to the American cause. A notable example was Dr. William White, chaplain to the Continental Congress and a trusted adviser of George Washington.

The declaration of peace in 1783 found the Episcopal Church disorganized. In Virginia and Maryland, the church was automatically disestablished and in some of the other Colonies became deplorably weak. The church in each state jealously preserved its independence and there was no bond of unity.

The first step toward creating such a bond was the publication in 1783 of a pamphlet entitled "The Case of the Episcopal Churches in the United States Considered," by William White of Philadelphia, but published anonymously and before peace was declared; it urged measures for the perpetuation of the ministry without waiting for the Episcopate, and outlined a general plan which embodied most of the essential characteristics of the diocesan and general conventions as adopted later. The moment the British authorities suggested peace, the pamphlet was withdrawn.

In Maryland, 1780, a conference was called, consisting of clergymen and laymen, who sent a petition to the legislature asking that the vestries be empowered to raise money for parish uses, by pew rents and other means. As it was essential to the petition that the organization have a title, the name Protestant Episcopal Church was suggested as appropriate—the term "Protestant" dis-

EPISCOPAL, CHURCH OF ENGLAND

tinguishing it from the Church of Rome, and the term "Episcopal" distinguishing it from the Presbyterian and Congregational bodies. This name was formally approved by a conference at Annapolis in 1783, and appears to have continued in use until definitely adopted by the General Convention of 1789.

While at the beginning of the Civil War the Southern dioceses met in Columbia, S. C., as the "Protestant Episcopal Church in the Confederate States," the break was not regarded as more than temporary, and at the General Convention at Philadelphia in 1865 the full number of states was retained in the roll call.

The first General Convention met in Philadelphia, September, 1785, with clerical and lay delegates present from the states of New York, New Jersey, Pennsylvania, Delaware, Maryland, Virginia, and South Carolina. A constitution was adopted, the Liturgy revised and an address to the Church of England adopted asking for the consecration of bishops for America.

The English bishops were unwilling to consecrate a bishop for America, owing to some of the changes which had been made in the prayer book. The Convention of 1786 complied with their requests, save in the case of the restoration of the Athanasian Creed, which was not included. A little later, Dr. James Madison was chosen Bishop of Virginia and consecrated in London.

The first twenty years of the nineteenth century are known as the period of painfully slow growth. Religious emotionalism ran riot; the Liturgy was regarded as formal; the sermons were more moral than Christian, and the Church was still regarded as British.

In 1789, the Constitution of the Church and the Prayer Book were revised, resulting in the union of hitherto divergent views; and Bishop Seabury in 1792 united with the other three bishops (Pennsylvania, New York and Virginia) in the consecration of Dr. Thomas Claggett as Bishop of Maryland, this being the first Episcopal consecration in the United States, and thus inaugurating the distinctively American Episcopate.

The Book of Common Prayer has been revised a number of times; the last complete revision was approved at the General Convention of 1928.

Doctrine

The Church maintains that the Holy Scriptures are the ultimate rule of faith. Her symbols of doctrine are the Apostles' and the Nicene Creed and the Thirty-nine Articles of the Church of England, except for such modifications as were made necessary by changed conditions after the War of Independence.

Its position rests upon the four foundation stones of the Chicago-Lambeth Quadrilateral—namely, the Historic Episcopate, the Holy Scriptures, the Apostles' and Nicene Creeds, and the two major Sacraments (baptism and the Supper of the Lord). The Church of England's Book of Common Prayer as revised by the General Conventions of 1892 and 1928 being the official formulary and standard of worship.

The Athanasian Creed, one of the symbols of the Church of England, was unanimously rejected by the Protestant Episcopal Church convention of 1789, chiefly because of its damnatory clauses.

As to its teachings, the Episcopal Church builds on three doctrines: The Mystery of the Holy Trinity, the Mystery of the Incarnation and the Mystery of the Atonement. The worship of the church is liturgical. A sacrament is, "An outward and visible sign of an inward and spiritual grace." In a certain sense, the great primary sacrament is the sacrament of the Incarnation. The other sacraments are but extensions of this great Mystery, and they minister to the Life which the Incarnate Christ bestows, e.g., in Holy Baptism. In the Holy Communion, bread and wine are given.

The subject of Christian Unity has been to the fore in the Episcopal church since the General Convention, which met in Chicago, and adopted as a basis of reunion four articles which were formulated in England in 1888 and have since been known as "The Lambeth Quadrilateral." They are as follows:

(a) The Holy Scriptures of the Old and New Testaments as "Containing all things necessary to salvation," and as being the rule and ultimate standard of faith.

(b) The Apostles' Creed as the baptismal symbol, and the Nicene Creed as the sufficient statement of the Christian faith.

(c) The two sacraments ordained by Christ himself—baptism and the Supper of the Lord—ministered with unfailing use of Christ's words of institution and of the elements ordained by Him.

(d) The historic episcopate, locally adapted in the methods of its administration to the varying needs of the nations and peoples called of God into the unity of His Church.

The doctrinal symbols of the Protestant Episcopal church, so far as the laity are concerned, are the Apostles' and Nicene creeds. The Thirty-nine Articles of the Church of England are, with some modifications, printed at the end of the American Prayer Book, but subscription to them is not required. The church expects of her members loyalty to her doctrine, discipline and worship, but allows considerable latitude in the interpretation of the creeds.

The Protestant Episcopal Church recognizes all who are lawfully baptized into the name of the Holy Trinity, as members of the Church, and further requires that all who have been baptized shall be brought to the bishop for confirmation but only after they have been adequately instructed in the Catechism. By a strict interpretation of an ancient rubric, only those who have been confirmed may come to the Holy Communion, but a more liberal view prevails in practice. Two sacraments only are recognized as generally necessary for salvation—baptism and the Supper of the Lord.

In the baptism of children, either immersion or pouring is allowed. The child must be presented by sponsors, who may be the parents and who shall answer for the child, accepting the Apostles' creed, with the implied promise that the child shall be trained to accept the pledges thus made.

For those who have not been baptized in infancy, reception into the church is by baptism—by whatever form preferred—and by acceptance of the Apostles' creed. For those who have been baptized, reception is by confirmation by the bishop.

EPISCOPAL, CHURCH OF ENGLAND

Organization and Government

Episcopacy—or Episcopalianism (as to government) is one in which one order of the clergy is superior to another; as bishops to priests and deacons, as contrasted to that form of church government named Presbyterianism (elders of equal rank).

The clergy of the Church of England are of three orders: deacons, priests, and bishops. Only the bishop can ordain and confirm or can consecrate churches. A bishop is given consecration at the hands of other bishops. The archbishop of Canterbury is the Primate of All England while the archbishop of York is the Primate of England. The archbishoprics of Canterbury and York form the administration districts. In both dioceses there are two convocations each with two houses, since the 13th century. These have an upper house that is composed of the archbishop and the bishops, and a lower house in which the representatives of the other clergy sit. The meaning of the convocations has changed in the course of the centuries. They meet regularly in recent times, and their discussions have great moral influence, although without the cooperation of the national power they cannot form legally binding decrees. Recently there has been added to the Convocation of Canterbury a house of the laymen, which may discuss all questions with exception of the questions of doctrine.

The system of ecclesiastical government of the Protestant Episcopal Church in America includes the parish or congregation, the diocese, the province, and the General Convention.

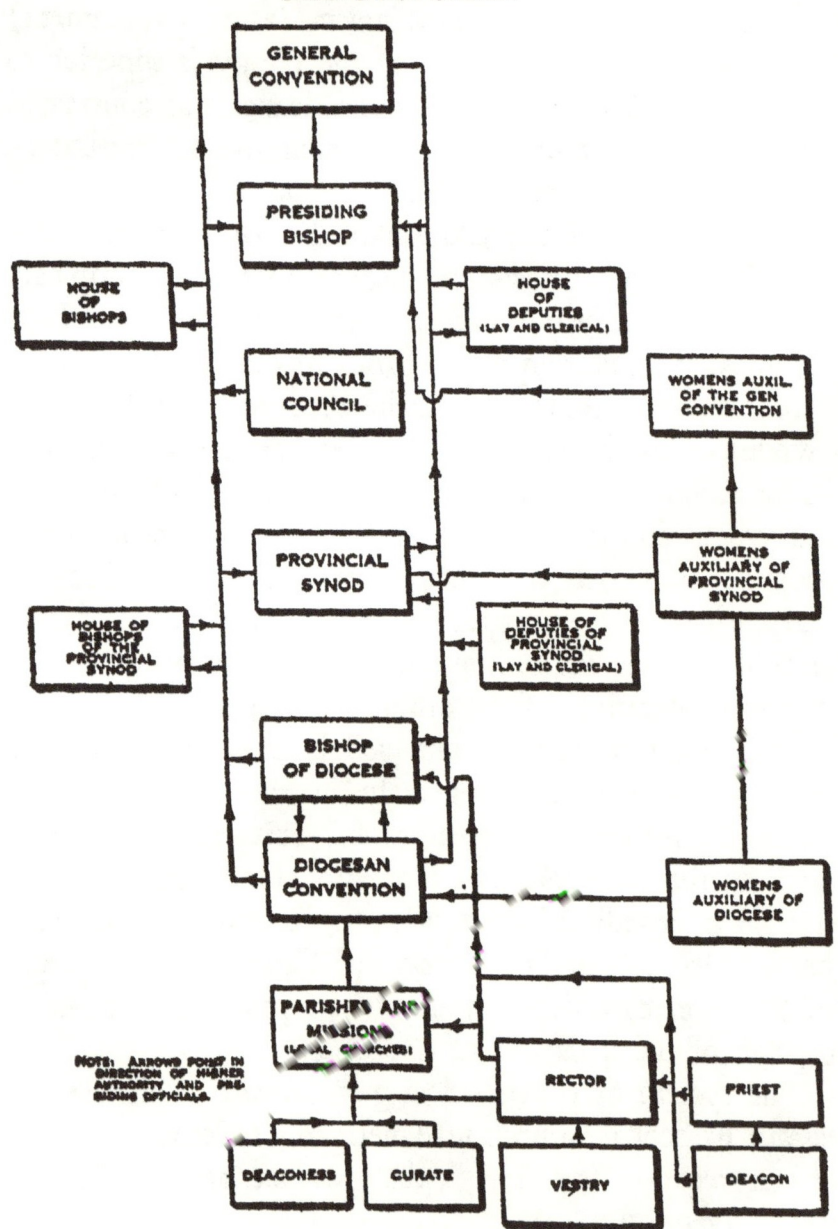

The unit of the Church is the diocese, presided over by its own bishop, who also has his diocesan council to coordinate with the National Council. The National Council is the executive agency for carrying out the will of the General Convention. The General Convention is composed of the two houses—The House of Bishops, and The House of Clerical and Lay Deputies.

A congregation, when organized, is "required, in its constitution or plan or articles of organization, to recognize and accede to the constitution, canons, doctrine, discipline, and worship of the church, and to agree to submit to and obey such directions as may be from time to time received from the bishops in charge, and council of advice."

The organization of the Protestant Episcopal Church (U. S. A.) is in general accord with the Mother Church of England.

The Episcopal church recognizes three orders in the ministry—Bishops, Priests and Deacons. Deacons must have reached the age of twenty-one. They cannot administer the Holy Communion and their special duty is to care for the sick and poor of the parish and preach only when licensed by the bishop. No one can be ordained a priest until he has been one year a deacon and is twenty-four years old.

Lay readers and deaconesses are appointed by the bishop or ecclesiastical authority of a diocese or missionary district to assist in public services and are under the control of the immediate ecclesiastical authority, and may not serve except as duly licensed.

Parish and Missions (Local Church or Congregation)
  Consists of the following:
    Rector (Spiritual Director who must be a priest.)
    Vestry (Directors of the Parish Corporation, whose powers are exclusive control of temporality only. They also hold the title to the property of the church.)
    Senior Warden (Appointed by the Rector, and acts as first Vice-President of the Vestry.)
    Junior Warden (Appointed by the Vestry, and acts as second Vice-President of the Vestry.)
    Clerk
    Treasurer
    Financial Secretary
    Women's Auxiliaries
    Men's and Women's Service Clubs
    Boys' and Girls' Service Clubs

The direction of spiritual affairs is exclusively in the hands of the rector. The number, mode of election, and term of office of wardens and vestrymen, with qualifications of voters, vary according to diocesan law. The election of officers, including the rector rests with the vestry as the elected representatives of the congregation. In some dioceses women are now permitted to vote for the vestry. The vestry is trustee for the property of the corporation.

The parish elects delegates to the Diocesan Convention. Wardens are delegates to the Diocesan Convention ex officio.

There must be at least six self-supporting parishes before a missionary district may become a diocese.

The election of the rector is according to diocesan law,

EPISCOPAL, CHURCH OF ENGLAND

and notice of election is sent to the ecclesiastical authority of the diocese. No election is valid without the consent of the bishop.

The parish (local congregation) elects the vestry and the vestry (representing the parish) elects the rector (usually for life).

Rectors of parishes are usually elected by the Vestry, though in some states the election must be ratified by the congregation and in all cases the assent of the bishop to the election must be obtained. The rector has sole charge of the spiritual concerns of the parish, subject to the godly counsel of the bishop; and he is entitled to the use and control of the church and church buildings.

The rector is removable by the bishop only. He is not responsible to the vestry on spiritual matters.

Diocese-Diocesan Convention

Next to the parish, comes the diocese, which is made up of the bishop or bishops, the clergy within the diocese and laymen elected by the parishes and missions of the diocese. The diocese is empowered to make assessments for the support of the episcopate.

The government of the diocese is vested in the bishop and the diocesan convention, the latter consisting of all the clergy, and of at least one lay delegate from each parish or congregation. This convention meets annually, and election of delegates to it is governed by the specific canons of each diocese. A standing committee is appointed by the convention to be the ecclesiastical authority for all purposes declared by the General Convention. This committee elects a president and secretary from its own body, and meets in conformity to its own rules; its rights and duties, except as provided in the constitution and canons of the General Convention, are prescribed by the canons of the respective dioceses.

In missionary districts the diocesan convention is generally called the Convocation and the standing committee is appointed by the bishop.

Diocese—Bishop of Diocese

A diocese includes not less than six parishes, and must have not fewer than six presbyters who have been for at least one year canonically resident within its bounds, regularly settled in a parish or congregation and qualified to vote for a bishop. Many states have been divided into several dioceses, New York and Pennsylvania, for instance, each now containing five separate bishoprics.

Sections of states and territories not organized into dioceses are established by the House of Bishops and the General Convention as missionary districts. These districts may be elevated into dioceses or may be consolidated with other parts of dioceses as new dioceses.

Dioceses and missionary districts are grouped into eight provinces. Each province is governed by a synod consisting of the bishops and of four presbyters and four laymen, elected by each constituent diocese and missionary district.

A bishop is a priest elected to that office by a diocesan convention and then approved by a majority of the standing committees of all the dioceses in the United States and a majority of the bishops having jurisdiction in the United States.

Diocesan bishops are elected by the clerical and lay members of the convention of the diocese, a majority of whom must sign the necessary testimonials. Three bishops are necessary to a valid consecration.

Missionary bishops are appointed in missionary districts by the House of Bishops, subject to confirmation, during the session of the General Convention, by the House of Deputies, and at other times, by a majority of the standing committees of the dioceses.

He is the administrative head and spiritual leader of his diocese. He presides over the diocesan convention, ordains deacons and priests, institutes rectors, licenses lay readers, and is required to visit every parish in his diocese at least once in three years. In case of the inability of a bishop to perform all the duties of his office, a bishop coadjutor may be elected in the same manner as the bishop, with the understanding that he shall have the right of succession to the bishopric. A suffragan bishop may be elected in the same way, when there is need of additional episcopal services. His authority is limited and he has not the right of succession.

No new diocese is allowed to be constituted except as provision is made for the support of the episcopate.

Lay readers and deaconesses are appointed by the bishop or ecclesiastical authority of a diocese or missionary district to assist in public services.

House of Bishops and House of Deputies of Provincial Synod

These act in similar capacity and relation to the Provincial Synod as do the higher House of Bishops and House of Deputies in relation to the General Convention.

Provincial Synod

It consists of a number of dioceses and missionary districts in a certain geographic area (there are eight in the United States).

Each provincial synod has its House of Bishops (which constitute all bishops in the particular province) and a House of Deputies (which consists of four priests and four laymen from each diocesan convention and three priests and three laymen from each missionary district).

It elects its own executive board which is called the Provincial Council of the Provincial Synod. This body has no legislative authority over its constituent dioceses. It elects members to the National Council.

National Council

The National Council was created in 1919, and conducts the missionary work of the church between the sessions of the General Convention. It also constitutes the Board of Directors of the Domestic and Foreign Missionary Society.

The council is composed of four bishops, four presbyters, and eight laymen, elected by the General Convention, and of one member elected by each of the provincial synods. The provincial representative may be either a bishop, presbyter, or layman.

One-half of the membership of this council is elected each three years. Also one bishop, priest or layman from each provincial synod is elected to this council for a three-year term and is designated as ex-official member. The executive officer of the National Council is elected bishop with the title of President of the National Council.

House of Deputies

The House of Deputies is composed of delegates elected from the dioceses, including for each diocese not more than four presbyters, canonically resident in the diocese, and not more than four laymen, communicants of the church, resident in the diocese. In addition to the delegates from the dioceses, each missionary district of the church within the boundaries of the United States is entitled to one clerical and one lay deputy, with all the qualifications and rights of deputies except the right to vote when the vote is taken by orders. The two houses sit and deliberate separately. On any question the vote of a majority of the deputies present is sufficient in the House of Deputies, unless some special cannon requires more than a majority, or unless the clerical or lay delegation from any diocese demands that the vote be taken by orders. In such case the two orders vote separately, each diocese having one vote in the clerical order and one in the lay order, a majority in each order of all the dioceses being necessary to constitute a vote.

House of Bishops

The House of Bishops includes every bishop having jurisdiction, every bishop coadjutor, every suffragan bishop and every bishop who by reason of advanced age or bodily infirmity has resigned his jurisdiction.

It meets annually and it elects its own officers. It also

elects missionary bishops. The House of Bishops is the final authority on doctrinal matters for the entire church.

Presiding Bishop

The ecclesiastical head of the church is the Presiding Bishop. Prior to 1804, this office was elective, but in that year the rule was adopted that the senior bishop in point of consecration, should be the Presiding Bishop. In 1919, the church decided to return to the earlier custom, and the House of Bishops, subject to the approval of the House of Deputies, was instructed to elect one of its members as Presiding Bishop, who would thereupon relinquish his diocesan responsibilities in order to devote himself to the general administration for a term of 6 years, then it was changed so that a presiding bishop holds office until he is 68 years old. This is the present method.

Under the constitution, the Presiding Bishop may be president of the National Council and is the executive head of the missionary, educational, and social work of the general church.

The Presiding Bishop is elected by the House of Bishops and ratified by the House of Deputies. He is responsible for consecrations to the episcopate and for all other matters concerned with the constitutional well being of the Church. He may preside over the House of Bishops and over the joint sessions of the convention.

General Convention

It is the supreme legislative authority of the Protestant Episcopal Church. It elects members of the National

EPISCOPAL, CHURCH OF ENGLAND

Council. The General Convention consists of two houses, the House of Bishops and House of Deputies (lay and clerical).

It meets every third year on the first Wednesday in October unless a different day be appointed by the preceding convention, and at the place designated by such convention, though the presiding bishop of the church has the power, in case of necessity, to change the place.

Prior to 1919 the church was without authority to act between General Conventions. This situation was remedied by the creation of the National Council, which now conducts the missionary work of the church between the sessions of the General Convention.

CHAPTER XII

LUTHERANS

Those adhering to the Lutheran doctrines are located, in the order of their numbers, in the following places: Europe, North America, Asia, Africa, South America, Islands. Their total number is approximately 4.1% of the world's and 12% of the total Christian population.

HISTORICAL SKETCH

Since the 16th century the name Lutherans has been used to designate those Protestants whose religious faith is based on the principles advocated by Martin Luther, although he opposed such a designation. When it became apparent to Luther that the reforms he desired could not be carried out in the Roman Catholic Church, he devoted himself to questions of faith rather than form in the new "Evangelical" churches that developed. His was the conservative attitude as distinguished from the views of the Reformed (Calvinistic) communions. His emphasis was upon the "responsibility of the individual conscience to God alone," with the Scriptures as the one standard for judging doctrines and institutions and the only necessary guide to truth. In addition to the Apostles', Nicene, and Athanasian creeds, accepted from the first, the principal statements of faith are found in Luther's two Catechisms, the Augsburg Confession, the Apology of the Augsburg Confession, the Schmalkald Articles, and the Formula of Concord. In these the fundamental doctrine is justification by faith. Baptism was counted necessary for regeneration, but no form of baptism was specified. As to manner of worship, Luther chose to retain altars, vestments, etc., and prepared an order of service liturgical in form. But no church is bound to follow any set order, and there is no uniform liturgy belonging to all branches of the Lutheran body. Characteristic features, however, are the important place given to preaching and the opportunity for congregational singing. Luther's own hymns, "Ein feste Burg" and many others, gave a special impetus to this custom. The celebration of the great Christian festivals has always been retained. Matters of administration and organization were worked out by others than the founder of the Evangelical Lutheran churches. To bring about order, superintendents over districts were appointed to work in cooperation with the secular rulers. In general, a synodical form of organization was developed, but the relations of individual churches to the synods and conferences rest with their own decisions and are controlled by circumstances. The unity of the Church is a unity of doctrine rather than of organization.

In Germany Lutheranism was in close association with the political life. In its early years there were many struggles to decide controversies within its own membership and to reach agreement with the Reformed churches. Temporal authorities took part in these matters. With doctrinal orthodoxy secured, a period of quiet followed, interrupted by the arousing influence of Pietism toward the end of the 17th century. When in 1817, under

Frederick William III of Prussia, a union between Lutheran and Reformed churches was at last accomplished and the resultant Church was adopted as the national Church, a large group remained outside the union and took the name Evangelical Lutheran Church of Prussia. They are also known as "Old Lutherans." In the unification of German culture under the National-Socialist (Nazi) rule, the church is included. In July, 1933, a national organization, the German Evangelical Church, was formed, including 29 separate state churches. Thus were consolidated all the Protestant bodies of Germany, both Lutheran and Reformed, except the small, scattered "Free" churches. All were to be united in a common creed, though each member church was to keep its own. Over the organization a Lutheran bishop should preside, and ecclesiastical legislation should be in the hands of a National Synod. The Nazi group, the "German Christians," with Dr. Ludwig Mueller as Reichsbishop, proceeded to develop a racial church, in which Aryan blood in one's veins was made a qualification for official position and a test of membership. Although the claim was made that organization alone was involved, it became apparent that the issues really concerned doctrines and the confession. A great controversy, led by 3,000 Protestant pastors, resulted. Another element was added when the "German Faith" movement, an evolved paganism, going back to the supposed cultural religion of the German race, began to demand legal recognition.

Outside of Germany the Lutheran Church is the established State Church of Denmark, Iceland, Norway, Sweden, Finland, Estonia, and Latvia.

LUTHERANS

The history of the Lutheran church in the Americas, both North and South, is largely the story of migrations from Lutheran countries. In South America, the Welsers from Augsburg sponsored a settlement in Venezuela in 1529. The colony, however, went the way of Spanish conquest. Likewise, in North America, Lutherans from the French colonies met Spanish conquest under Menendex, who boasted that he had come to the Americas to hang and behead all Lutherans.

Up to the middle and, indeed, the latter part of the eighteenth century, the history of the Lutherans in America is not alone the history of the migration of peoples but the history of the individual congregations and pastors as well. Even before the middle of the eighteenth century, steps were taken looking toward the organization of pastors and churches into conferences and synods.

Lutheran settlers came to Manhattan Island from the Netherlands in 1623. The first congregation of the present St. Matthew's Lutheran Church of New York was formed in 1648; but it was antedated by a congregation established, 1638, by Swedish settlers at Fort Christina (Wilmington) on the Delaware river. There the first Lutheran Church building in the country was dedicated in 1646, English Lutheran services were first held in Germantown and Philadelphia in 1694. Early in the 18th century exiles from the Palatinate settled in the Middle Atlantic region and established German Lutheran churches in New York, Pennsylvania, Delaware, and Maryland. The Salzburger migration to Georgia introduced Lutheranism into the South. In the 18th century organization of the churches was begun by Heinrich Melchior Muhlenburg, who brought about the formation of the first synod in the country, in Pennsylvania, in 1748. The Synod of New York and adjoining states followed, in 1786; that of North Carolina, in 1803. With the settlement of the West and the Northwest, a great number of small synods were formed by people speaking different languages, but these were in time absorbed into larger synods. In almost all cases, the congregation is regarded as the unit of organization and the seat of authority.

The extraordinary growth of the Lutheran church in America was due primarily to Lutheran immigration, and to the activity on the part of the different synods aimed to reach all new immigrants. During the 19th century, these immigrants in large numbers, came to America, establishing German, Swedish, Norwegian, Danish, Icelandic, Finnish and other language settlements, largely in the central, northwestern and western parts of the continent.

Doctrine

The Lutherans in general accept the canonical Scriptures of the Old and New Testaments as the inspired Word of God and as the only infallible rule and standard of faith and practice. They assert the responsibility of the individual conscience to God alone, in all matters of faith and life. All church power inheres in the Word of God. They accept and confess the three ecumenical creeds: Namely, the Apostles', the Nicene, and the Athanasian.

LUTHERANS

They accept and hold the Unaltered Augsburg Confession as the correct exhibition of the faith and doctrine of the Evangelical Lutheran church, founded upon the Word of God. None reject any of the other symbolical books of the Evangelical Lutheran church, namely, the Apology of the Augsburg Confession, the Schmalkald Articles, the Large and Small Catechisms of Luther, and the Formula of Concord. Many accept all of these. All accept and use Luther's Small Catechism.

The cardinal doctrine of the Lutheran system is justification by faith alone in Jesus Christ. It acknowledges the Word of God as the only source and infallible form of all church teaching and practice. The Lutheran faith does not center in the doctrine of the sovereignty of God or in the church, but rather in the Gospel of Christ for fallen men. The church's unity is a unity of doctrine, and its independence is an independence in regard to government.

Lutherans reject both transubstantiation, as held by the Roman Catholic church, and consubstantiation, as attributed to them by some writers. Lutherans believe that the real body and blood of the Lord Jesus Christ are present in, with and under the earthly elements in the Lord's Supper, and that these are received sacramentally and supernaturally. The church believes in infant baptism, and baptized persons are regarded as having received from the Holy Spirit the potential gift of regeneration, and are members of the church, though active membership follows confirmation. To the Lutherans, the mode of baptism is considered of secondary importance.

The Lutheran Church is conservative in spirit and holds to all the teachings and customs of the ancient church which are not in conflict with the scriptures.

Divisions of the Lutherans

The following churches, although they are distinct and independent bodies, have substantially the same doctrines and church government as the general Lutheran churches.

*Joint Synod of Ohio, 1818; *Buffalo Synod, 1858; *Eielsen Synod, 1846; †Missouri Synod, 1847; †Joint Wisconsin Synod, 1850; *Ohio Synod, 1854; *Augustina Synod, 1860; *Danish Church, 1872; *Finnish Apostolic Church, 1872; †Negro Mission, 1877; *Icelandic Synod, 1885; *Suomi Synod, 1890; *Emmanuel Synod; *Jehovah Conference, 1893; *United Danish Church, 1896; *Lutheran Free Church, 1897; *Lutheran Brethren, 1900; *Finnish National, 1900; †Slovak Synod, 1902; Norwegian Lutheran Church, 1917; †Norwegian Synod, 1919; *United Lutheran Church in America, 1918.

United Lutheran Church in America

The United Lutheran Church in America is the direct successor and heir to three of the Lutheran bodies—the General Synod of the Evangelical Lutheran Church in the United States of America, the General Council of the Evangelical Lutheran Church in North America, and the United Synod of the Evangelical Lutheran Church

---

*Churches cooperating in the National Lutheran Council.
†Churches constituting the Synodical Conference.

in the South. These bodies were merged into the United Lutheran Church in America in 1918.

National Lutheran Council

History. The National Lutheran Council is not a synod or church body but an association of church bodies through their duly appointed representatives. It is an agency through which general bodies or synods of the Lutheran church cooperate under regulations guaranteeing to each the rights, privileges and immunities of a free church body. Its most important work, since its organization in 1918, for statistics, publicity, and representation, has been done in behalf of European relief.

Membership in the national council includes ministerial and lay delegates elected by the state conferences, and also delegates from the local associations. Membership in an association is generally regarded as esssential to good and regular standing in the denomination. No association or conference, or national council, however, has any ecclesiastical authority. That is vested solely in the council called by the local church for a specific case, whose existence terminates with the accomplishment of its definite purpose. The result is that there is no appeal from one court to another, although an aggrieved party may call a new council, which, however, has no more authority than its predecessor.

Synodical Conference of North America

History. In the early part of the nineteenth century, an effort was made by King Frederick William III of

Prussia to unite the Lutheran and Reformed churches. To him it seemed an easy matter to combine "the two slightly divergent confessions;" but, in the study of the sources of confessional divergence which naturally followed, and particularly in the attempt to furnish a uniform liturgy for both bodies, old convictions were intensified, and lines of demarcation which had been gradually fading out were revived. Many of the Lutherans refused absolutely to recognize the union, formed separate congregations, and carried on an active controversy against what they recognized as a gross form of ecclesiastical tyranny.

During the following twenty years, the situation grew more strained, and, as Lutheran immigration to the United States began, several of these communities removed to this country.

In 1847, twelve congregations, twenty-two ministers and two candidates for the ministry united in forming the "German Evangelical Lutheran Synod of Missouri, Ohio and other states." Under the constitution adopted, only those ministers whose congregations had entered into membership with the synod, and the lay delegates representing those congregations, were entitled to suffrage. All the symbolical books of the Lutheran Church (Book of Concord 1580) were regarded as "the pure and uncorrupted explanation and statement of the Divine Word." All joint work and worship with churches of divergent profession were disapproved. Purely Lutheran books were to be used in church and schools. A permanent, not a temporary or licensed ministry was affirmed, and, at the same time, freedom of the individual congregation was recognized, the synod having no authority over it.

Under the leadership of Walther, the Missouri doctrine gained acceptance, and as one synod after another was formed on the same general basis, it seemed advantageous to effect some form of union. At the time of the organization of the General Council in 1866, several of these synods were invited to participate, but those which held the stricter doctrine could not accept the position taken by the new body. The next few years emphasized anew the advantage of union, and, in 1872, in Milwaukee, Wisconsin, the Evangelical Lutheran Synodical Conference of America was formed.

Their basis of union is not so much a matter of common ecclesiastical organization, as of a common church life, and particularly of doctrinal purity, and uniformity of practice.

Doctrine. In doctrine, the Synodical Conference recognized but one standard, to which there must be absolute accord, namely, the Holy Scriptures as interpreted by the Book of Concord of 1580, including a text and commentary upon the three ecumenical creeds—the Apostles', the Nicene and the Athanasian; and upon the six Lutheran confessions—the Augsburg Confession, the Apology of the Augsburg Confession, the Schmalkald Articles, Luther's Smaller and Larger catechisms, and the Formula of Concord. This unwavering confessionalism is the most treasured possession of the Conferences, and to its faithful adherence to this policy it attributes its remarkable growth.

Independent Congregations
(Not affiliated with any synod)

Besides the Congregations in the synods, there are a number of independent Lutheran Congregations which do not belong to any synod. In most cases, the reason is not so much doctrinal, but simply a love of independence, groups merely desiring to hold their church services independently of any other organization. Usually, however, there have been some one or more "points" of doctrine on which they have disagreed, resulting in certain groups withdrawing and forming independent congregations. Not infrequently the pastor of an independent church is himself a member of some synod.

ORGANIZATION AND GOVERNMENT

Those adhering to the Lutheran doctrines fall into three main groups—first, evangelical Germany, Poland, Russia, Lithuania, Czechoslovakia, Austria, Hungary, Rumania, Yugoslavia, France and Holland; second, a group of other nations which have established the Lutheran church as the state church—Denmark, Iceland, Norway, Sweden, Finland, Esthonia and Latvia; third, the United States of America and Canada. The whole comprises the largest confessional group in the non-Roman Evangelic Christendom.

Lutheran Churches in America are diametrically opposed to any state influence aside from constitutional rights of freedom to worship. Nevertheless, organization has taken place in all Lutheran bodies, whatever the parent country whence they came, along lines having at

LUTHERANS

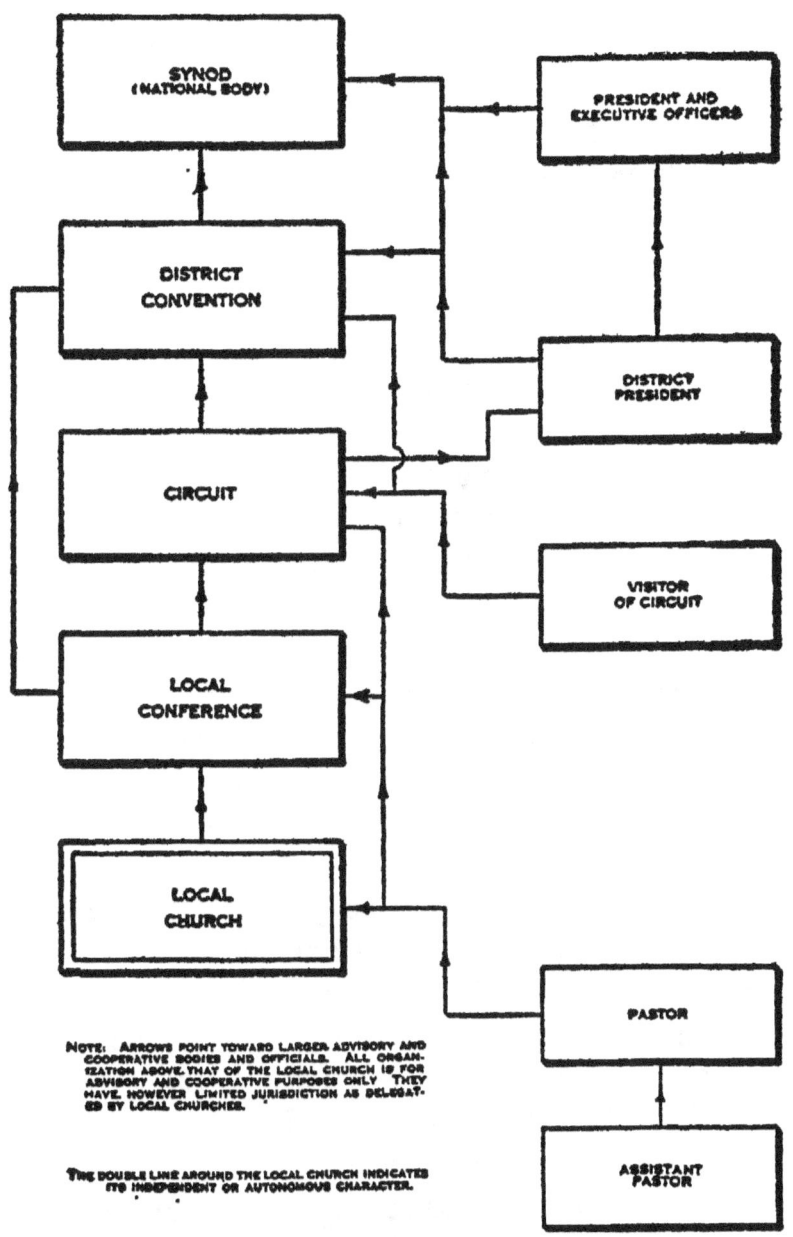

least general resemblance to the arrangements adopted for the conduct of political government.

Among Lutherans the distinction between the laity and the clergy or ministry rests solely upon the orderly exercise of a function which is necessary to the being and continuing life of the church—namely, the preaching of the Gospel and the administration of the sacraments. This is committed to the ministry, and in reference to the exercise of this function all ministers are equals; and besides this there is no power which the minister as such can claim the right to exercise, whether he be called bishop, priest, minister, or pastor. All of these are designations of office, not of necessary orders in the ministry or among the faithful. All powers held by officials of local, district or national conferences are limited to those delegated to them by the local congregation.

The congregation is composed of the people and the pastor. The pastor is elected and called by the voting members of the congregation, without any time limit. The congregation has the power, however, to terminate the relationship, but it may not depose the pastor from the ministry of the church.

In every Lutheran Church body in America the congregation is acknowledged as the primary body and the unit of organization. All authority belongs to the congregation together with the pastor, except such as is delegated by constitutional agreement to the larger organization. The internal affairs of the congregation are administered by a church council consisting of the pastor and lay officers. These officers are elected by the congregation, and in many instances a number of them are called elders and others deacons; where this is the case the elders together with the pastor have charge of the spiritual concerns and the deacons of the temporal affairs of the church. In other cases there are no elders, but deacons only. There are also trustees who have charge of the property. These are laymen and may or may not be members of the church council.

To every congregation belongs inherently the right of representation and also the right of entering into relations with other congregations one with it in faith for the purpose of promoting common interests and activities. From these principles result wider organizations.

Organization above the congregation assumes various forms in the several church bodies. In some cases the next higher judicatory is the synod. The synods are composed of the pastors of the congregations and of lay representatives, one for each congregation or each pastoral charge, and they have only such powers as are delegated to them by the congregations under the provisions of the synodical constitution. In other cases there are districts or conferences which are territorial, which are similarly composed and exercise within their respective bonds the rights and duties constitutionally assigned to them. Some of these have limited powers of legislation, while others are chiefly consultative and advisory.

The interests entrusted mainly to the general bodies are those pertaining to general education, publication, and missionary activities.

There is general agreement that the seat of authority

and power is vested in the local congregation. The differences which are found as between the districts of the several bodies and as between the general bodies themselves in regard to the powers exercised by them are to be explained, in part at least, by the processes of organization. In some cases the intermediate organizations (conferences, districts, synods) were first organized and later the general bodies, the process being from below upward; in such cases the powers of the intermediate bodies are relatively larger. In other instances the general bodies were organized with a small beginning, and as they grew were divided, thus forming the intermediate organizations from above downward. In instances of this kind the powers of the intermediate organizations are relatively less.

Local Church

    Consists of the following:

        Pastor
        Board of Deacons
        Board of Trustees
        Finance Committee
        President or Chairman of the Congregational Meeting
        Secretary
        Treasurer
        (The above may constitute the Church Council—the Pastor serves ex officio.)
        Auxiliary Organizations
          Sunday School
          Ladies Aid
          Altar Guild

LUTHERANS

Young People's Societies
Men's Club

The local church or parish is in itself autonomous in all matters of organization and government. Each local congregation governs completely what officers are needed and by vote elects all officers.

When a local church (or congregation) joins a larger or national body, it subscribes to the confessions as outlined by that body and is amenable thereto. Each congregational organization calls its own pastor. Dismissal may be by call of another congregation, false doctrine or ungodly life.

A mission church or congregation usually acts under the general supervision of a national body or may act solely under a local autonomous church.

All organizations other than that of the local church or congregation are for administrative and advisory purposes only.

The right of choosing and calling ministers and schoolteachers and of electing all other officers of the congregation shall ever be vested in the congregation and shall never be delegated to an individual or to a minor body or circle within the congregation.

Local Conference

It generally consists of the pastors and parochial school teachers in the designated or particular local conference (geographic area).

Three or more local churches or parishes constitute a local conference.

The chief purpose of a local conference is for educational advantages and cooperative administrative functions.

The Circuit

It consists of a pastor and one lay delegate from each parish or local church within the designated or particular circuit.

Two or more local conferences constitute a circuit. The chief activity of the circuit is along educational and informative lines.

Any authority which it may have is delegated to it by the local churches.

It functions chiefly in administrative and advisory capacity.

District Convention

It consists of a pastor and one lay delegate from each local church or parish within the designated or particular district (geographical arrangement). It meets every two years, except the year when the General Body or Synod meets (every three years).

A district is presided over by a president who has two vice-presidents and an indefinite number of visitors.

Any authority which it may have is delegated to it by the local churches.

It acts in an advisory capacity.

Synod or National Convention

It consists of one pastor to each Circuit and one lay delegate from each Circuit according to rotation or seniority of the parishes (local churches).

The Synod meets once every three years and in area includes all of the districts in the United States.

It is presided over by a president and a board of directors.

Any authority which it may have is delegated to it by the local churches.

It acts in a cooperative and advisory capacity.

CHAPTER XIII

METHODISTS

Those adhering to the Methodist doctrines are located, in the order of their numbers, in the following places: North America, Europe, Islands, Asia, Africa and South America. Their total number is approximately 1.5% of the world's, and 4% of the total Christian population.

Historical Sketch

The Methodist organizations developed from the movement started in England by the teaching of John Wesley. He, his brother Charles, George Whitefield, and others belonged to a group at Oxford which, in 1729, began meeting for religious exercises. From their resolution to conduct their lives and religious study by "rule and method" they and their societies were given the name "Methodists." The leaders of the movement were ordained ministers of the Church of England; neither of the two Wesleys ever broke the connection with that church, but they were barred from speaking in many pulpits of the Established Church, where dignity and conservatism were cherished.

As converts were received, they were organized into societies for worship, and, as the work expanded, class meetings were formed for the religious care and training of members. Wesley's catholicity was so broad that he was not greatly concerned whether the books he reprinted for his people were by Roman Catholics or Unitarians, so long as they tended to their religious edification. It was his hope that his movement would be the nucleus of a reunited Christendom, and it was with sorrow he saw forces which he could not control carrying his followers into permanent separation. In fact, "In John Wesley's idea, Methodism was not to found a church. He permitted no Methodist service to be held in church hours. The change came when the number of persons excluded from the Communion and treated as lost by the clergy, grew so great that it was inconvenient for them to use the best hours of the Sunday for the services to which they were attached. The title, 'Methodists,' was not of his choosing—it was given by Oxford students because of the strict life of Charles Wesley and his band in the University, but he took it up as a matter of course."

They preached in houses, barns, open fields, wherever an audience could be reached. Societies were formed, class meetings of the converts were held, lay preachers were trained and given "circuits," of several congregations each, to serve. When they were changed about from one appointment to another, the system of itinerancy had its beginning. When the Articles of Religion were drawn up at the first annual conference (1744), they were based to a considerable extent upon the Thirty-nine Articles of the Church of England, but great emphasis was laid upon repentance, faith, and sanctification. The privilege of full, free salvation was offered everyone. Whitefield could not agree to this and became the leader of the Calvinistic Methodists.

Though the Wesleys lived and died in full ministerial relations with the Church of England, serious differences arose between the church and the Methodists. In 1745, John Wesley wrote that he was willing to make any concession which conscience would permit, in order to live in harmony with the clergy of the established Church, but that he could not give up the doctrines he was preaching, dissolve the societies, suppress lay preaching, or cease to preach in the open air. For many years, he refused to sanction the administration of the sacraments by any except those who had been ordained by a bishop in the apostolic succession, and he himself hesitated to assume authority to ordain.

Not until 1784 did Wesley take the authority of ordaining others. Then he ordained Dr. Thomas Coke before sending him to superintend the societies in America. The Methodists in England adopted a legal constitution in 1784, and in 1791, after the death of Wesley, they were formally separated from the Church of England. In both England and America a number of secessions have given rise to branch organizations, differing from their parent groups in some matter of church government, but never in doctrine. Reunions of branches have been effected from time to time. In the British Isles the Methodist New Connection was the first group to form a separate branch. Then followed the Primitive Methodists, the Bible Christians, the Protestant Methodists, the Wesleyan Methodist Association, and the Wesleyan Reformers. In 1857 the last three formed a union as the United Methodist Free Churches, and in 1907 these were incorporated with the Methodist New

Connection and the Bible Christians as the United Methodist Church. Finally, in 1932, the Wesleyan Methodists, the Primitive Methodists, and the United Methodists were gathered together again into one great church under the United Conference of Methodist Churches. John and Charles Wesley visited America in 1735, as spiritual advisers to General Oglethorpe's colony in Georgia; but the actual beginnings of the Methodist Church in America were in New York after 1766, when Philip Embury, a Wesleyan local preacher, who had come with a company of emigrants from Ireland, began preaching. In 1769 Wesley sent several itinerant preachers into the new field, among them Francis Asbury. In 1773 ten preachers met for the first annual conference in the New World. In 1784 Dr. Coke and Asbury were denominated bishops of the Methodist Episcopal Church. To the Order of Worship and Articles of Religion, prepared by Wesley, an article pledging allegiance to the United States was added. In 1830, after controversy over lay representation in Conferences and other questions, the Methodist Protestant Church was formed. It has no bishops or presiding elders. The Wesleyan Methodist Connection was organized at Utica, N. Y., in 1843, in a strong antislavery protest. After the Civil War many returned to the parent body, but the denomination continued in nonepiscopal organization.

The question of slavery had become so critical an issue by 1845 that the Southern Conferences met in Louisville, Kentucky, to adopt a plan of separation from the General Conference. The result was the independent career of the Methodist Episcopal Church, South. From this body in 1852 a group withdrew to form the Congregational Methodist Church. Other branches of the Methodists in the United States who have rejected the episcopal mode of government are the Free Methodist Church of North America, and the Primitive Methodist Church, introduced by emigrants from England. In the early years of the 19th century Negro Methodists in the Middle Atlantic States withdrew from the congregations where they had membership and formed denominations of their own. In 1870 the Colored Methodist Episcopal Church became a separate body approved in the General Conference of the Methodist Episcopal Church, South. In the United States, as in Great Britain, there has for some time been a strong tendency to reunite the various denominational bodies. In Canada in 1925 the Methodist Church united with the Presbyterian and Congregational Churches to form the United Church of Canada.

Doctrine

In theology, the Methodist churches are Arminian and their doctrines are set forth in the Articles of Religion (1744) formulated largely from the Thirty-nine Articles of the Church of England (reducing their number by omission and abbreviation to twenty-five); Wesley's published sermons contain forty-four discourses and his Notes on the New Testament. These emphasize belief in the Trinity, the fall of man, his need of repentance, freedom of the will, sanctification, future rewards and punishments, and a sufficiency of the Scriptures for salvation.

While laying due emphasis upon the doctrines commonly called orthodox, Methodism has placed the chief stress from the beginning upon Christian character and service. It has been strong in its defense of the Protestant principles of the right to read the Bible, the right of private interpretation and of freedom of conscience, and it has also been disposed to allow large liberty in non-essentials. In opposition to Methodism, is the Calvinistic theology.

A summary of Methodist doctrines is as follows: The unity of the Godhead, and the co-equal divinity of the Father, the Son and the Holy Ghost; the death, resurrection, ascension, and intercession of Jesus Christ; salvation by faith; the sufficiency of divine inspiration of the Holy Scriptures. Methodism maintains man's total depravity, through the fall of Adam, and his utter inability, unless aided by divine grace, to take one step towards his recovery; but it holds that this grace is free, extending itself equally, by virtue of the atonement, to all the children of men. Methodism teaches also that it is the privilege of believers in this life to reach that maturity of grace, and that conformity to the divine nature, which cleanses the heart from sin and fills it with love for God and man. This they call Christian perfection, a state which is attainable through faith in Christ.

Two sacraments are recognized—Baptism and the Lord's Supper. Baptism is administered both to infants and to adults. As to mode, sprinkling is preferred; though, in the case of adults, choice of sprinkling, pouring or immersion is given.

Divisions of the Methodists

The following churches, although distinct and independent bodies, have doctrines and church government substantially the same as those of the Methodist Episcopal church.

United States

Methodist Episcopal Church; Methodist Episcopal Church, South, 1845; Methodist Protestant Church, Baltimore, 1830; Wesleyan Methodist, Utica, N. Y., 1843; Free Methodist, New York, 1850; Primitive Methodist Church, U. S. A.; Congregational Methodist Church; New Congregational Methodist Church, Georgia, 1881.

Great Britain

The Methodists in England adopted a legal constitution in 1784 and in 1791, after the death of Wesley, they were formally separated from the Church of England.

In the British Isles the Methodists New Connection was the first group to form a separate branch. Later the Primitive Methodists and the Bible Christians, were organized. In 1847 the Protestant Methodists, the Wesleyan Methodist Association and the Wesleyan Reformers were united as the United Methodist Free Churches. In 1907 these Free Churches were incorporated with the Methodist New Connection and the Bible Christians as the United Methodist Church. In 1932 the United Conference of Methodist Churches was formed.

United States
(Colored)

African Methodist Episcopal, Pennsylvania, 1783; African Methodist Episcopal Zion, New York, 1796; Union American Methodist Episcopal, Delaware, 1813; Colored Methodist Protestant, Maryland, 1840; African Union Methodist Protestant, Pennsylvania, 1866; Reformed Zion Union Apostolic, Virginia, 1869; Colored Methodist Episcopal in America, 1870; African American Methodist Episcopal, Baltimore, 1873; Reformed Methodist Union Episcopal, South Carolina, 1885.

ORGANIZATION AND GOVERNMENT

The form of church government, while following the general rules laid down by Wesley, is somewhat different in England and in America. In England, the conference remains supreme and the superintendency is not emphasized; in America, the leading Methodist bodies are Episcopal in their form of government. This Episcopal form of government, while not corresponding exactly to that of the Episcopacy of the Church of England, is a decided factor in church life.

In each country, but especially in America, considerable opposition has developed at different times in connection with some features of the parent body, and divisions have resulted. In every case, however, the general principles of the founders have been preserved, and notwithstanding the various separations, the Wesleyan Methodist Connection in England and the Methodist Episcopal Church in the United States remain the

HIS MANY MANSIONS

METHODIST EPISCOPAL CHURCH
ORGANIZATION DIAGRAM

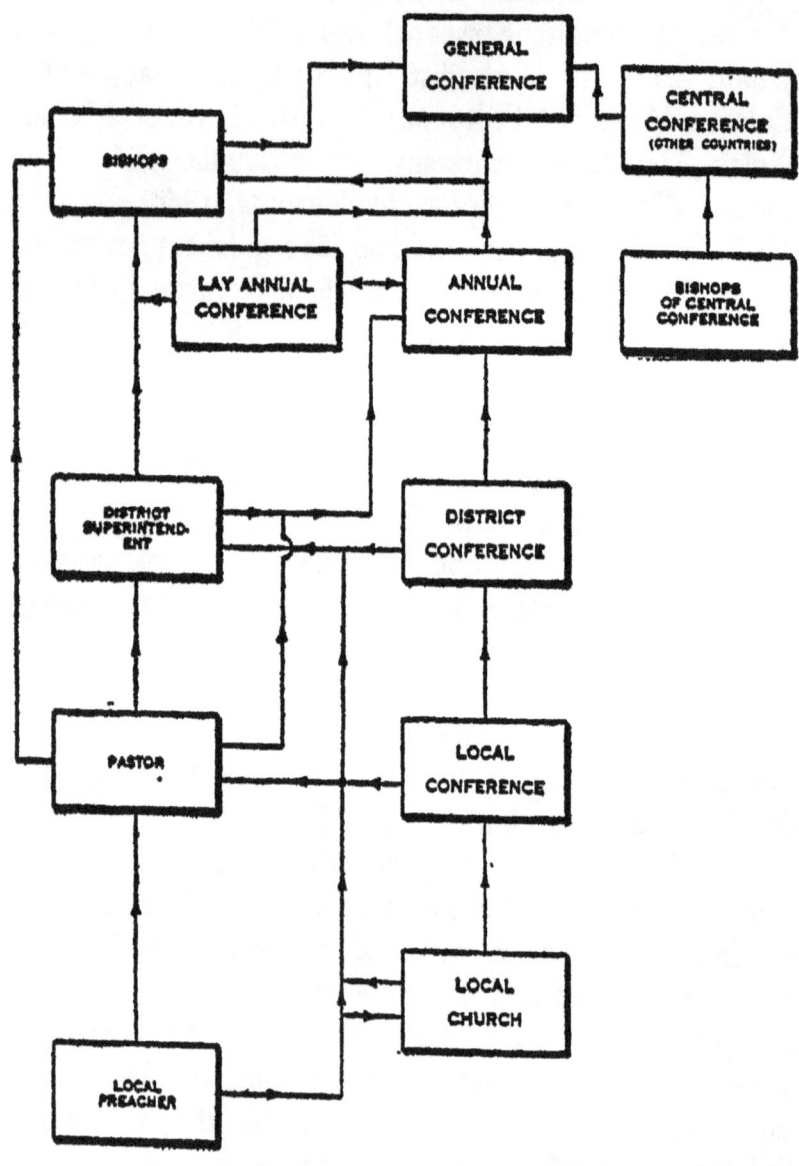

NOTE: Arrows point toward presiding officials or higher jurisdiction.

METHODISTS

strongest representatives of the movement initiated in Oxford nearly two centuries ago.

It is to be noted that the influence of the Methodist doctrine and church organization has not been confined to those bodies which have adopted the name "Methodist," but has been manifest in the development of a number of bodies which use modified forms of the episcopal, presbyterial, and congregational systems of government.

The ecclesiastical organization of the Methodist Episcopal Church includes the local church, the ministry, and the system of conferences.

The local church is ordinarily a single congregation with its own pastor (a separate pastor). To meet the needs of small congregations, unable to support a separate pastor, two or more congregations may be united in a circuit, all being under the care of one pastor. Each pastorate, whether it be a single congregation or a circuit, is termed a "charge," and appointments by the annual conferences are to charges, not to churches.

The membership of the local church is distinctly a lay membership; ministers are members of the annual conferences. Lay members are of two classes—full members and preparatory members. Full members are those who have been formally received into membership on recommendation of the official board, or the leaders' and stewards' meeting, and with the approval of the pastor. Preparatory members (formerly called probationers) are those who, after they have been instructed so as to be "wise unto salvation," may, on recommendation of the boards of the church, and with the approval of the pastor, be received into full membership. They include all applicants for church membership, and under a recent revision of the rules, all baptized children. The preparatory relation is obligatory upon all candidates for full membership, the length of time, formerly six months, now being indefinite. Preparatory members are entitled to all church privileges, but may not vote or be voted for, and are included in all statistics of church membership, except that in the case of baptized children only those are included who have been enrolled in the classes for instruction. Full lay members, both male and female, have a vote in all church matters, and are eligible to local church offices and to membership in the quarterly and district conferences and in the General Conference, but not in the annual conferences. Women are now eligible for the ministry as local preachers, but not for conference membership.

For instruction and spiritual help probationers and members are assigned to classes, over which leaders are appointed. The business of the local church is generally conducted by an official board, while the property is held by trustees. The charges also have Sunday schools, Epworth Leagues, aid societies, and such other organizations as may be desired.

The regular ministry of the Methodist Episcopal Church includes two orders—deacons and elders. Under certain conditions, however, it has been the policy of the church to use laymen as exhorters and local preachers. A local preacher is usually a layman adjudged to have "gifts, grace, and usefulness," who is licensed to preach by the district conference or the quarterly conference in whose jurisdiction he resides, but is not expected to give up his ordinary business. He becomes a member of the quarterly conference, is under its supervision, and his license must be renewed annually, or he may be ordained as deacon, or elder, or both. The term, "local preacher" is applied also to unordained men "on trial" in the annual conferences, to ordained deacons, and to traveling ministers who have been located by their conference.

The regular ministry, generally spoken of as traveling preachers or itinerant ministers, is presented in the official minutes of the church under two heads—on trial and members of annual conferences.

Under the first head are included candidates for the ministry who have the status of local preachers. Candidates are certified by a district or quarterly conference, and are received into an annual conference "on trial." After two years, on passing an examination in a prescribed course of study, they are eligible to ordination as deacons and to election to full membership in the conference. They have authority to solemnize matrimony, administer baptism, and assist in the administration of the Lord's Supper. After serving as deacon for two years and having completed the four years' course of study, they are eligible to election by conferences and to ordination by a bishop as elders. Some qualifications or allowances are made in the case of candidates for the ministry who come from theological seminaries under the auspices of the Church or from other ecclesiastical bodies.

Deacons and elders are members of annual conferences and are classed as effective, supernumerary, or retired.

Elders have power to consecrate the elements of the Lord's Supper and are eligible to appointment as district superintendents, to a pastoral charge, or to some other church office, or for election as bishops. Originally, pastors, or "itinerants," as they were termed, moved every six months, and then every year. In 1900 the time limit was removed entirely. The usual length of a pastorate, however, continues to be two or three years. Supernumeraries and retired ministers are elders or traveling ministers, who, temporarily or permanently, are classed as incapacitated for effective service. A "located" traveling minister is one whose membership in the annual conferences is discontinued, although he retains his ordination and holds the position of a local elder or deacon in a quarterly conference.

Bishops, also called general superintendents, are elders elected by the General Conference and consecrated by three bishops, or by one bishop and two elders. They preside at general conferences and at annual conferences, according to special assignments by the board of bishops, make annual appointments to pastoral charges, ordain deacons and elders, and have general oversight of the religious work of the church.

The system of conferences includes quarterly, district, mission, annual, and general conferences.

The quarterly conference, identical in membership with the official board in each pastoral charge, is the highest authority in the station or circuit for the purpose of local administration.

Each church is practically independent in the conduct of its own financial affairs, though subject to the general ecclesiastical system. The salary of a pastor is fixed by an estimating committee of the quarterly conference of the charge he serves; that of a district superintendent, by the stewards of his district; that of a bishop, by the Book Committee of the church. The Book Committee divides the total amount necessary for episcopal salaries and expenses and for the expenses of general and judicial conferences among the annual conferences, they in turn informing each church of its share.

The Local Church

Consists of the following:

> Pastor
> Retired Ministers
> Detached Ministers
> Local Preachers
> Board of Trustees
> Board of Stewards
> Unit Leaders
> Church Committees
> Sunday School
> Church Brotherhood
> Young People's Organizations
> Ladies Aid Society
> Missionary Societies

The pastor acts as President of the Official Board (which consists of trustees, stewards, all ministers and heads of all departments within the local church).

The pastor is appointed by the bishop in annual conference; the class leader, by the pastor; local preachers and exhorters are licensed by the quarterly conference; and other officers are elected or nominated by the various departments or by the pastor, but are confirmed by the quarterly conference.

A pastor may be either a deacon or an elder or in preparation for ordination.

There are also deaconesses, who are generally unmarried women, and work under the direction of the general Deaconesses Board. They act as assistants to the pastor in the local charge.

The Local or Quarterly Conference

When the district superintendent or his appointee meets with the local church heads (who only are officially entitled to vote) they then become a local conference.

A local conference is held for the purpose of hearing reports from all department heads, electing boards and committees and transacting such business as may properly come before this controlling body of the local church.

In connection with a local conference there is a lay electoral conference which meets in quadrennial session for the purpose of electing lay delegates to the General Conference—the number corresponding to the ministerial delegates to the General Conference.

The District Conference

This is composed of all ministers serving in the district and one lay member from each church of the district, also deaconesses working within the bounds of the district. It

METHODISTS

is secondary to the Annual Conference. It has no authority to assign ministers.

It meets in the mid-year between the sessions of the Annual Conference. It acts in an advisory capacity. The district superintendent is the presiding officer, unless the bishop be present. In general its duties are nearly identical with those of the quarterly conference, though it reviews the mutual relations of charges as well as their internal affairs.

District Superintendent

District superintendents, or presiding elders, as they were formerly termed, are elders appointed by the bishops for limited terms, to represent them in the care of the interests of the church in particular districts. They form the members of the bishop's cabinet to advise of the appointment of ministers, etc. They also have supervision over the work in their respective districts. They can make appointments of ministers and effect exchanges between pastors in the interim between sessions of the Annual Conference subject to the approval of the bishops. They also preside at the quarterly and district conferences. Only an elder is eligible to the office of district superintendent.

The Annual Conference

It consists of all ministers of the Methodist Episcopal Church serving charges within the bounds of the Annual Conference (geographic area), together with the retired ministers and detached members of the Conference and also one official lay delegate from each pastoral charge.

Annual Conferences vary in number of pastoral charges from approximately fifty (smaller conferences) to more than five hundred (larger conferences).

The resident bishop of the area presides over the Annual Conference. There may be several Annual Conferences within an episcopal area. Each bishop has a cabinet in each of the Annual Conferences which is composed of the district superintendents and bishop.

The Annual Conference is an administrative and not a legislative body. Its membership is confined to traveling ministers, whether effective, supernumerary, or retired; and all members, together with those on trial, are required to attend. It receives reports from pastors, district superintendents, and statisticians; the bishop ordains candidates for deacons, and elder's orders, and appoints the ministers to their charges; ministerial delegates are elected to the General Conference; and questions of discipline are decided. A lay electoral conference, composed of one lay delegate from each pastoral charge within its bounds, meets in connection with the annual conference just preceding the General Conference, in order to elect lay delegates to that conference.

The Lay Annual Conference

Representation is based on one layman from each pastoral charge (local church) within the bounds of the Annual Conference. It has co-ordinate voice in all affairs of the Annual Conference with the exception of purely ministerial functions, such as the ordination, advancement and appointment of ministers.

There are an equal number of lay delegates to ministerial delegates from the Lay Annual Conference elected to seats in the General Conference. Its purpose is to make the whole polity more democratic and give lay members equal voice with the ministerial members in the management and direction of the affairs of the church.

Bishops

A bishop is a general superintendent in the Methodist Episcopal Church and is elected by the two-thirds majority vote of the General Conference. His function is to act co-ordinately in presiding over the General Conference. He has supervision over the area to which he is assigned by the General Conference.

A bishop makes annual appointments of all ministers in the Annual Conferences over which he presides. He also visits the district conferences and institutes and conventions within his area. He is responsible only to the General Conference.

Bishops of Central Conferences function in a similar manner to the Central Conferences as the bishops in the United States function in connection with the General Conference.

Bishops also ordain deacons and elders and have general oversight of the religious work of the church. A bishop is an elder set apart for a specific task. Bishops are elected by two-thirds majority vote of the General Conference (which is composed of an equal number of lay and ministerial delegates). The candidate is then consecrated to the office of bishop.

Central Conference

In countries outside of the United States the highest body of the Methodist Episcopal Church is called a Central Conference, corresponding to the General Conference in the United States. Each Central Conference, however, is autonomous within its own country.

The General Conference

The General Conference is the highest body in the church and is the general legislative and judicial body. It is presided over by the bishops, who, however, are not delegated members thereof, but are members ex officio, with limited privileges. It authorizes the organization of annual and mission conferences, and fixes their boundaries; it elects the bishops, official editors, publishing agents, book committee, the corresponding secretaries and board of managers of the administrative societies of the church, the members of the different boards of trustees, and book committees.

It is a delegated body composed of an equal number of ministerial (bishops excluded) and lay delegates from all the Annual Conferences in Methodism. The number of delegates is based on the number of members in the Annual Conferences. The ratio now being one lay and one ministerial delegate to every forty-five members of each Annual Conference.

Various general boards, which are created by the General Conference, e.g., Board of Foreign Missions, World Service Commission, Board of Education, etc., act continuously.

The General Conference elects and ordains all bishops

and assigns them to their respective areas (assignments for a period of four years with possible reassignment for a like period).

The General Conference may authorize the organization of an Annual Conference. Approximate membership of the General Conference is between eight and nine hundred and is presided over by a different bishop each day it is in session.

The bishops are the presiding officers but have no vote. It meets once every four years; the session continuing through the month of May.

CHAPTER XIV

PRESBYTERIANS

Those adhering to the Presbyterian doctrines are located, in the order of their numbers, in the following places: Europe, North America, Islands, Africa, Asia, South America. Their total number is approximately 1% of the world's and 3% of the total Christian population.

Historical Sketch

As the Lutheran churches represent those features of the Reformation emphasized by Luther, so the Presbyterian and Reformed churches represent those emphasized by Zwingli and Calvin.

Scotland is the only country where Presbyterianism is established by law. Presbyterian churches are the direct heirs of Calvinism in doctrine and government.

The Presbyterian churches first influenced by Calvin were those of Geneva and of the Huguenots. In the Netherlands the Protestant church was Presbyterian in government, but independent only in the 19th century, when the state church became autonomous. By the middle of the 16th century Presbyterian sentiment was strong in England. The Westminster Assembly, convened by Parliament (1645-49), had no lasting authority in England, but set the standards of subsequent Presbyterians. The English Presbyterians after Cromwell have been a small body, mostly supported by the Scots, and in 1876 a union of English congregations of the United Presbyterian Church of Scotland with the Presbyterian Church in England was set up, called the Presbyterian Church of England. The Church of Scotland (Kirk of Scotland) succeeded to all the unsequestrated properties of the pre-Reformation Church, but before long a group led by Richard Cameron, called first the Cameronians or Covenanters, and finally (1743) after long persecution, the Reformed Presbyterians, seceded. Most of these joined (1876) with the Free Church of Scotland. The Associate Synod, or Secession Church of Scotland, was formed by Ebenezer Erskine and his adherents, who withdrew from the established church in 1733, after trouble over patronage. Division in the Associate Synod itself was caused by disagreement over a burgess oath. "Burghers" and "anti-Burghers" resulted; and out of these, by division in each party, grew "New Lights," who held modern ideas on limiting the duties of civil magistrates, and "Old Lights," and conservative minorities. They came together in 1820 in the United Secession Church, which in 1847 joined with the Relief Church to form the United Presbyterian Church. The Relief Church was a secession movement from the Church of Scotland—which started after the expulsion of Thomas Gillespie and aimed to relieve "Christians oppressed in their Christian privileges." Its presbytery dated from 1761. Most extensive of all the losses in membership was that of the Great Disruption of 1843, out of which emerged the Free Church of Scotland, releasing itself from all benefits of the established church but continuing in the same doctrine and discipline.

In 1900 the Free Church and the United Presbyterian Church were joined in one United Free Church of Scotland. Irish Presbyterianism began in the early 17th century and it has always centered in Ulster (the greatest number of church members in Northern Ireland are Presbyterians). The Presbyterian Church of Ireland (organized finally 1840) is the principal body. The great Protestant church of Wales, the Calvinistic Methodist Church, is a Presbyterian church. Canada received Presbyterianism from Scotland. After 1760, presbyteries were built up in different provinces. These separate bodies were organized into four large ones in 1870, and the Presbyterian Church of Canada was formed. This church joined with the Methodist and Congregational church of the country in 1925 in the establishment of the United Church of Canada. Not all the Presbyterian churches in the land entered the union. Within most of the early settlements of the English colonies of North America Presbyterians were found, especially among the colonists from Scotland. Churches grew up in Virginia, Maryland, Delaware, New England, New Jersey, and Long Island, before 1683, when the Reverend Francis Makemie, from Ireland, started organization among them. The first presbytery was formed at Philadelphia in 1706; a synod was constituted in 1716. New England, from 1775 to 1782, had its own synod. In the 18th century, American Presbyterians divided temporarily over the question of revival and evangelism, the "Old Side" rejecting them, the "New Side" encouraging them. Before the Revolution the Presbyterians set up a college to educate ministers, the College of New Jersey, now Princeton University. After the Revolution a united Presbyterian church was formed, its first general assembly meeting in Philadelphia in 1789. A Plan of Union with the Congregational associations of New England existed from 1792, until 1837, when the "Old-School" party of the Presbyterians, favoring separate denominational agencies for missionary and evangelistic work, prevailed. The Presbyterian Board of Foreign Missions was then established. By 1810 a secession had taken place in Kentucky, and the Cumberland Presbyterian Church had resulted. In 1837 the "New-School" party adopted a "Declaration" at Auburn, New York, and a year later organized their own assembly. Because of their vigorous opposition to slavery, a defection of Southern Presbyterians from their ranks took place in 1858, and the United Synod of the Presbyterian Church was formed.

When in 1861 the Old-School assembly passed resolutions of loyalty to the Federal government, the Presbyterian Church in the Confederate States of America was established by secession from its body. Joined by the United Synod in 1864, this church of the South in 1865 changed its name to the Presbyterian Church in the United States. To it were added the synods of Kentucky and Missouri. The Old and New Schools accomplished a reunion by 1869. The Cumberland Presbyterian Church, with the exception of a seceding minority, again became a part of the main body in 1906, and the next year the Council of Reformed Churches in the United States holding the Presbyterian System was organized. The branch of the Welsh Calvinistic Methodists in the United States was the next to unite, in 1920, with the principal Presbyterian body, the Presbyterian Church in the United States of America. As yet no satisfactory plan has been found for uniting in one this great church of the North and the main body of Presbyterians in the South, although joint meetings of the General Assemblies of the two were held on special anniversary occasions, in 1888 and 1897. In the South, Negro Presbyterians have had an independent synod since 1897; there is also a Colored Cumberland Presbyterian Church (1869), which was not affected by the union of the Cumberland Presbyterians with the United Presbyterians (1903).

The United Presbyterian Church of North America resulted from the union (1858) of the churches in the United States representing the Associate Synod (Secession) and Associate Reformed Synod (Secession and Covenanter) of Scotland. The Associate Synod of North America (or the Associate Presbyterian Church), is that part of the church tracing descent from Erskine's secession in 1733 in Scotland. A very conservative church is the Associate Reformed Presbyterian Church, a secession (1822) from the Associate Reformed Synod. A direct American descendant of the Reformed Presbyterians of Scotland (Cameronians) is the Reformed Presbyterian Synod (1809). This split in two (1833) on the question of the propriety of the participation of Christians in political affairs. By far the greater number of American Presbyterians belong to the Presbyterian Church in the United States of America, the descendant of the first presbytery of Philadelphia. There is a constant tendency

PRESBYTERIANS

among Presbyterians towards reunion in America as well as abroad.

Doctrine

Presbyterianism is characterized by belief in the Bible as the sole rule of faith and conduct, by the careful preservation of the sacraments of baptism and the Lord's Supper, by a rigorous opposition to civil interference in ecclesiastical affairs, and by thorough education of the ministers. English-speaking Presbyterianism has for its standards of doctrine the Westminster Confession of Faith and the Larger and Shorter Catechisms.

Applicants for church membership are generally examined by the session as to their Christian life and belief, but are not required to assent to the creed of the church.

These were first adopted in 1729. As a whole, these standards are distinctly Calvinistic. In fact, it can be said that the controlling idea of the Presbyterian or Calvinistic system or thought, both theoretically and practically, is the doctrine of the unconditioned sovereignty of God. By this sovereignty is meant the absolute control of the universe in all that it contains, whether visible or invisible, by the one supreme, eternal, omniscient, omnipresent and omnipotent spirit, for wise, just, holy and loving ends, known fully alone to Himself.

This divine sovereignty finds expression in the sovereignty of the Word of God as the supreme and infallible rule of faith and practice. The Presbyterian system accepts and incorporates, as a perpetual binding obligation, only those principles and regulations which can be proved to have a divine warrant.

The church also declares that all persons dying in infancy are included in the election of grace, and are regenerated and saved by Christ through the spirit, "Who works when and where and how He pleases."

The usual form of baptism is sprinkling, both for infants and unbaptized adults, on confession of faith. The invitation to the Lord's Supper is usually general for all evangelical Christians.

They emphasize the sovereignty of God in Christ and in the salvation of the individual; affirm that each believer's salvation is a part of the eternal divine plan; that salvation is not a reward for faith, but that both faith and salvation are gifts of God; that man is utterly unable to save himself; that regeneration is an act of God and of God alone; and that he who is once actually saved is always saved.

The Directory of Worship makes no restriction as to place or form. The church insists upon the supreme importance of the spiritual element, and leaves both ministers and people at full liberty to worship God in accordance with the dictates of their own conscience. The sacraments are administered by ministers only, and ordinarily only ministers and licentiates are authorized to teach officially.

Divisions of the Presbyterians

The following churches, although they are distinct and independent bodies, have doctrines and church government substantially the same as those of the general Presbyterian bodies:

Presbyterian Church in the United States of America,

1788; Associate Synod of North America (associate Presbyterian Church), 1801; Cumberland Presbyterian Church, 1810; Associate Reformed Presbyterian Synod, 1822; Reformed Presbyterian Church (old school), 1833; General Synod, 1833; United Presbyterian Church of North America, 1858; Presbyterian Church in the United States (South), 1861; Colored Cumberland Presbyterian Church, 1869.

Organization and Government

Presbyterianism is the system of church organization based upon administration by a series of representative courts composed of presbyters, clerical and lay. The term Presbyterianism is derived from the Greek meaning "an Elder" or "Presbyter." It holds a middle ground between the other great types of church polity found among Protestant Christian churches, Episcopacy and Congregationalism. The one spiritual order of the church is composed of the presbyters (or elders), all of equal status, divided according to function into ministers and ruling elders. The presiding officer of any church court is primus inter pares (first among equals). The minister's duties are to teach, to preach, and to administer the sacraments. The elders, chosen by the congregation from among their own membership, are associated with the minister in the conduct of the spiritual life of the church. Usually, in addition, there are deacons to administer the benevolent funds and trustees to take charge of church property. The court of the congregation is the session or Kirk session, consisting of the minister, who presides, and the ruling elders, ordained to assist him in

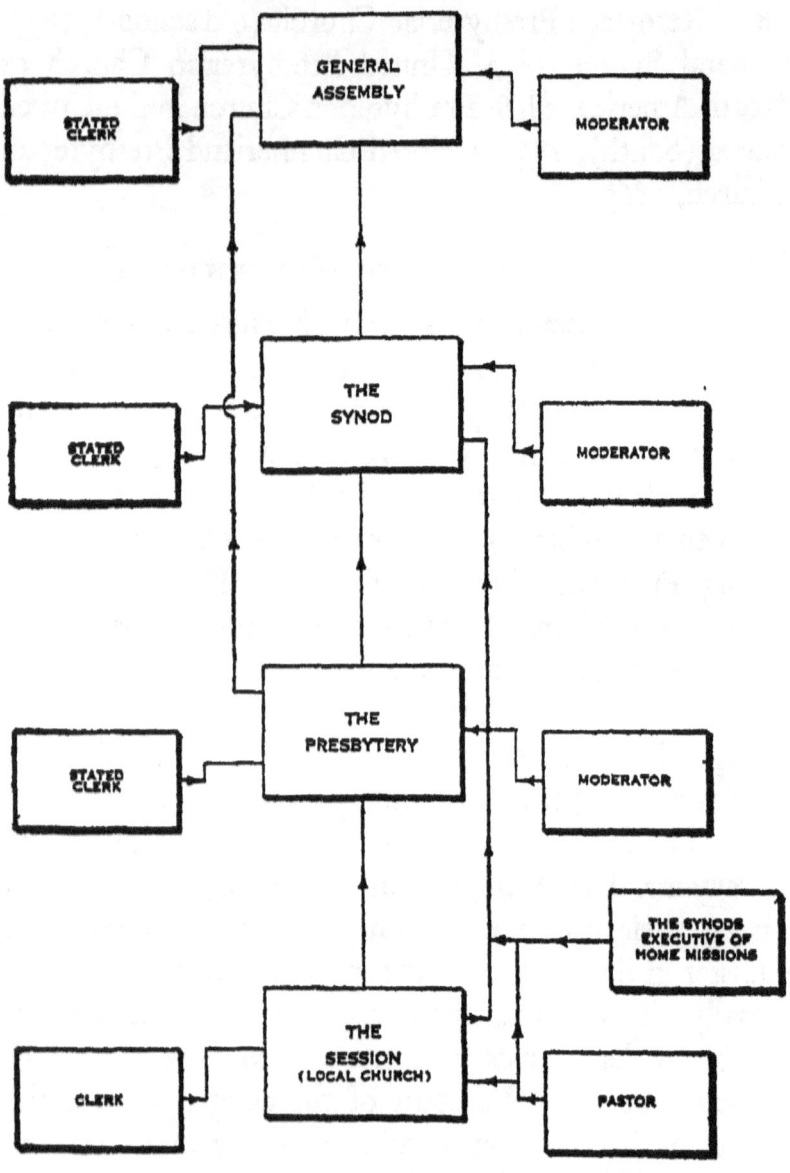

matters of discipline and direction. Appeal from this court may be made to the presbytery, which includes all the ministers from the congregations in a given area and one or more elders from each of the congregations. The presbytery alone holds jurisdiction over the ministers in its area. It alone can ordain ministers, and the call of a minister to any church must be confirmed by the local presbytery. A stated number of presbyteries are represented by ministers and chosen elders in the next higher, or provincial, court, the synod. In it are considered matters referred to its attention by the presbyteries. The national court and ordinary court of appeal is the general assembly, but three-fourths of the presbyteries agreeing are the final authority of a Presbyterian church. The general assembly is composed of a given number of delegates, ministers and elders, from each presbytery; its presiding officer, elected at its annual meeting and called the moderator, is official head of the church. The hierarchy of representative courts of the Presbyterian churches in the United States of America corresponds generally to the local, state, and national organizations provided in the American Constitution.

The Local Church

Consists of the following:

> Pastor
> The Session (Composed of Elders)
> Board of Trustees
> Board of Deacons
> Superintendent of Sunday School

Missionary Societies
Young People's Groups
Men's Club
Ladies Aid Societies

The pastor, elders and deacons as officers of each local church must subscribe to the Confession of Faith of the Church (national body) but it is not necessary for individual members to subscribe.

The Session, consisting of chosen elders is the official governing body of the local church in spiritual matters, subject to the Confession of Faith. Its members are elected by the local congregation as a whole and its number depends on the size of the church.

The pastor acts as moderator of the Session. Each local church usually initiates the calling of the pastor, who to be eligible, must have completed certain designated educational requirements. The pastor ordains elders and deacons after they have been chosen or elected by the congregation.

The Board of Trustees and the Board of Deacons are concerned chiefly with the temporal affairs of the local church.

All members of the church in good standing vote for the elders and deacons and in the calling (election) of the pastor. In the election of trustees, contributing members of the congregation may vote as well as members of the church.

All self-supporting churches have complete control over their property, while the property of the missionary churches is controlled by the Presbytery.

PRESBYTERIANS

The Presbytery

This consists of at least three ministers and one ruling elder from each local church.

It meets semi-annually or oftener as local conditions warrant. It examines, licenses and ordains candidates for the ministry and issues calls from the various local churches to pastors elect.

It acts as a first general appeal court to the Session or congregation. Appeal may be had from the Presbytery to the Synod or General Assembly.

The Moderator of the Presbytery is chosen each year to officiate for one year.

The Synod

It is composed of at least three Presbyteries. It comprises a geographic area usually according to state boundaries. It meets annually.

It supervises the work of the Presbyteries in its area, and also reviews the records of the Presbyteries and has the power to establish new Presbyteries, with the approval of the General Assembly. It acts as a cooperating agency between the various Presbyteries within its boundaries.

In more populous synods, delegates are elected from the Presbytery to the synod, in proportion to membership. In less populous synods each minister and each church has a place in Synod meetings.

The Moderator of the Synod is chosen each year to officiate for one year. The Stated Clerk is usually elected for a period of three years and is generally re-elected.

The General Assembly (National Body)

It is composed of an equal number of clerical and lay commissioners from each Presbytery on the basis of one minister and ruling elder for every twenty-four ministers in the Presbytery or fraction over half.

It meets every year and has legislative, executive and judicial functions. It reviews the records of each Synod.

It acts as a final appeal court from Presbytery or Synod.

The Moderator of the General Assembly is chosen each year to officiate for one year. The General Assembly elects a General Council to administer the affairs of the church between the meetings of the General Assembly. It also elects Benevolence Boards for the maintenance of religious education of missionary churches.

The General Assembly is the final court of decision for all controversies respecting doctrine and discipline and erects new synods. Its decision is final, except in matters involving the amendment of the constitution of the Church. Judicial cases not affecting the doctrine or constitution of the Church terminate with the synod as the final court of appeal; all others terminate with the General Assembly.

CHAPTER XV

ROMAN CATHOLIC CHURCH

Those adhering to the Roman Catholic doctrines are located, in the order of their numbers, in the following places: Europe, North America, South America, Islands, Asia, Africa. Their total number is approximately 17% of the world's, and 52% of the total Christian population.

HISTORICAL SKETCH

The Holy Catholic Apostolic Roman Church, more generally known as the "Roman Catholic Church," includes that portion of the Christian church which recognizes the bishop of Rome as pope, the vicar of Christ on earth, and the visible head of the church. It dates its origin from the selection by Jesus Christ of the Apostle Peter as "chief of the Apostles," and it traces its history through his successors in the bishopric of Rome.

Until the tenth century, practically the entire Christian church was recognized as one. Divergent views on various matters, particularly the doctrine of the Procession of the Holy Ghost, and the primacy of the bishop of Rome, culminated in the eleventh century in a separation between the Western and Eastern sections, now known as the Roman Catholic Church and Eastern Orthodox (Catholic) church, respectively.

The first Catholic congregation in the territory now

constituting the United States was founded at St. Augustine, Florida, in 1565, although Catholic services had been held on the soil of Florida long before that date.

Missionaries in connection with Coronado's exploring expedition in 1540, preached among the Indians of New Mexico, but they soon perished. After the founding of Santa Fe, the second oldest town in the United States, missionary work was more successful and many tribes of Indians accepted the Catholic faith. On the Pacific coast, Franciscans accompanied expeditions to California, about 1600, and on the Atlantic coast, French priests held worship on Neutral Island, on the coast of Maine, in 1609, and three years later on Mount Desert Island. Jesuit missions were begun on the upper Kennebec in 1646.

The history of the Catholic church among the English colonists began with the immigration of English and Irish Catholics to Maryland, in 1634, and the founding of the town of St. Mary's in that year. Religious toleration was from the beginning the law of the colony; but in later years, the Catholics were restricted and were disfranchised, and the restrictions were not entirely removed until after the War of the Revolution.

Following the war, however, religious liberty was not established by all the colonies at once, but the recommendation of the Continental Congress, in 1744, "that all former differences about religion or politics—from henceforth cease and be forever buried in oblivion," had its effect, and some of the colonies promptly removed the existing restrictions on the Catholics, admitting members of that church to all rights of citizenship.

Religious equality, however, became universal and complete only after the Philadelphia Convention of 1787, in which the present Constitution of the United States was adopted. During the discussion of the Constitution, a memorial was presented by the Reverend John Carroll, appointed (1784) superior of the missions in the United States; this undoubtedly contributed to the adoption of the provision of the sixth article which abolishes religious tests as a qualification for any office or public trust, and of that portion of the first amendment which says: "Congress shall make no law respecting an establishment of religion, or prohibiting the free exercise thereof."

The Revolutionary War left the Catholic church in America without any immediate hierarchical superior. The vicar apostolic of London held no intercourse with the church in America and refused to exercise jurisdiction in the United States. After considerable investigation and delay, the Propaganda proposed the name of John Carroll as the superior or perfect apostolic of the church in the thirteen original states, with the power to administer confirmation. This nomination was confirmed and was followed by a decree making the church in the United States a distinct body from that in England.

As the elementary school system developed in the American Colonies it was under the control of Protestants, who introduced Protestant forms of religious observance. The Catholics objected to conditions which constrained their children to attend, or take part in, non-Catholic services or instructions. The result was the absolute separation of public education from the control of any religious body. Modern Catholicism really begins with the Protestant Reformation. It took some years for the reform party within the Church to gain control which was finally accomplished by the Council of Trent and by the Jesuits.

Doctrine

The Roman Catholic Church bases its doctrines upon the canonical books of the sacred Scriptures, explaining and supplementing them by tradition expressed in written documents.

In 1870 the Vatican Council defined as a dogma of faith the infallibility of the pope, and that the Church members submit themselves in matters of faith and morals to the absolute authority of the pope. This infallibility is afforded to the pope when he speaks "ex cathedra" in matters of faith and morals, and in general to ecumenical councils of which there have been 21 to date. From this comes the Church's attitude toward the Bible, of which she reserves the sole right of interpretation.

The infallibility of the pope includes the means of grace, and the power to absolve sinners. The prime means of grace are the seven sacraments, which actually confer God's grace on the faithful. The chief sacrament is the Eucharist, in which the bread and wine become in substance the body and blood of Jesus Christ. By the sacrament of orders the clergy is set apart from the laity or the great body of believers. To the clergy is reserved the power to perform and confer the sacraments (except baptism), including penance, in which the Catholic confesses his sins and is absolved from them by a priest.

The clergy has complete control of church affairs, the bishops being deputies of the pope in their dioceses, the priests of their bishops in the parishes.

Supernatural powers of the clergy (e.g., in the sacraments) are conferred unconditionally by God, hence their personal qualifications and behavior do not affect the validity of the sacraments.

The Church teaches that the ultimate fate of every man lies in heaven or hell. By obedience to her (Roman Catholic Church) a man may be sure he will attain heaven. Those who die in grievous unrepented sin are sure of going to hell. To gain heaven the soul burdened with venial (pardonable, excusable) sin must be purified in Purgatory, from which the Church grants partial relief by indulgences. The dead in purgatory may be assisted by the prayers of the living. In its dogmatic system the Roman Catholic Church compels her people to believe without question: the dogmas are said to be of faith.

An important feature of the canon law is the dispensations, which is the permission granted by a competent authority, to do something not permitted ordinarily by the Church. These regulations are in force for all members of the Church, but there are however, many local differences in Church administration, in ceremonial, and in discipline. The most significant difference is one of Rite. A rite is that complex of customs and rules which has grown up within a Christian people more or less isolated from other peoples. The vast majority of Roman Catholics belong to the Latin rite prevalent in central and western Europe, in the Americas, and in the missions. In the Latin rite the clergy are celibate and the language of the Liturgy (Mass) is Latin. Other rites are principally found in Eastern Europe and the Near East. Some of them have married clergy; most of them have liturgies quite different from that of the Latin rite. None of them uses Latin; and many of them have their own hierarchy, headed by a metropolitan or patriarch who is responsible to the pope. The most important of these churches are the Ruthenian, the Armenian, the Italian, Greek, the Rumanian, the Melchite, and the Maronite rites.

The Apostles' creed, the Nicene Creed, and the Athanasian Creed are regarded as containing the essential truths accepted by the church. A general formula of doctrine is presented in "Profession of faith," to which assent must be given by those who join the church. It includes the rejection of all such doctrines as have been declared by the church to be wrong, a promise of obedience to the church's authority in matters of faith, and acceptance of the following statement of belief:

"One only God, in three divine Persons, distinct from and equal to each other—that is to say, the Father, the Son, and the Holy Ghost; the Catholic doctrine of the Incarnation, Passion, Death and Resurrection of our Lord Jesus Christ; the personal union of the two natures, the divine and the human; the divine maternity of the most holy Mary, together with her most spotless virginity; the true, real and substantial presence of the Body and Blood, together with the Soul and Divinity of our Lord Jesus Christ, in the most holy Sacrament of the Eucharist; the seven Sacraments instituted by Jesus Christ for the salvation of mankind: that is to say, Baptism, Confirmation, Eucharist, Penance, Extreme Unction, Orders,

Matrimony; Purgatory, the Resurrection of the Dead, Everlasting Life; the Primacy, not only of honor, but also of jurisdiction, of the Roman pontiff, successor of St. Peter, prince of the apostles, vicar of Jesus Christ; the veneration of the Saints and of their images; the authority of the Apostolic and Ecclesiastical Traditions, and of the Holy Scriptures, which we must interpret, and understand, only in the sense which our holy mother, the Catholic Church, has held, and does hold; and everything else that has been defined, and declared by the Sacred Canons, and by the General Councils, and particularly by the holy council of Trent and delivered, defined, and declared by the General Council of the Vatican, especially concerning the Primacy of the Roman Pontiff and his infallible teaching authority."

The sacrament of baptism, "cleanses from original sin," is administered to infants or adults by the pouring of water and the pronouncement of the proper words. Baptism is the condition for membership in the Roman Catholic Church, whether that sacrament is received in infancy or in adult years. At the time of baptism, the name of the person is officially registered as a Catholic and is so retained unless, by formal act, he renounces such membership.

Confirmation is the sacrament through which "the Holy Spirit is received," by the laying on of hands of the bishop, and the anointing with the holy chrism in the form of a cross. The Eucharist is "the sacrament which contains the Body and Blood, Soul and Divinity, of the Lord Jesus Christ, under the appearance of bread and wine." It is usually to be received fasting, and is given to the laity only in one kind—the form of bread. Penance is a sacrament in which the sins committed after baptism are forgiven. Extreme Unction is a sacrament in which the sick who are in danger of death receive spiritual succor by the anointing with holy oil and the prayers of the priest. The sacrament of Orders, or Holy Orders is that by which bishops, priests, and other ministers of the church are ordained and receive power and grace to perform their sacred duties. The sacrament of Matrimony is the sacrament which unites the Christian man and woman in lawful marriage, and such marriage "cannot be dissolved by any human power."

The chief commandments of the church are: To hear Mass on Sundays and Holy days of obligation; to fast and abstain from meat on the days appointed; to confess at least once a year; to receive the Holy Eucharist during Easter time; to contribute toward the support of pastors, and to observe the regulations in regard to marriage.

Organization and Government

The organization of the Roman Catholic Church centers in the Bishop of Rome as pope, and his authority is supreme in matters of faith and in the conduct of the affairs of the Church. Next to the pope is the College of Cardinals, who act as his advisers and as heads or members of various commissions called Congregations, which are charged with the general administration of the Church. These never exceed 70 in number, and are of three orders: Cardinal deacons, cardinal priests, and cardinal bishops. These terms do not indicate their

ROMAN CATHOLIC CHURCH

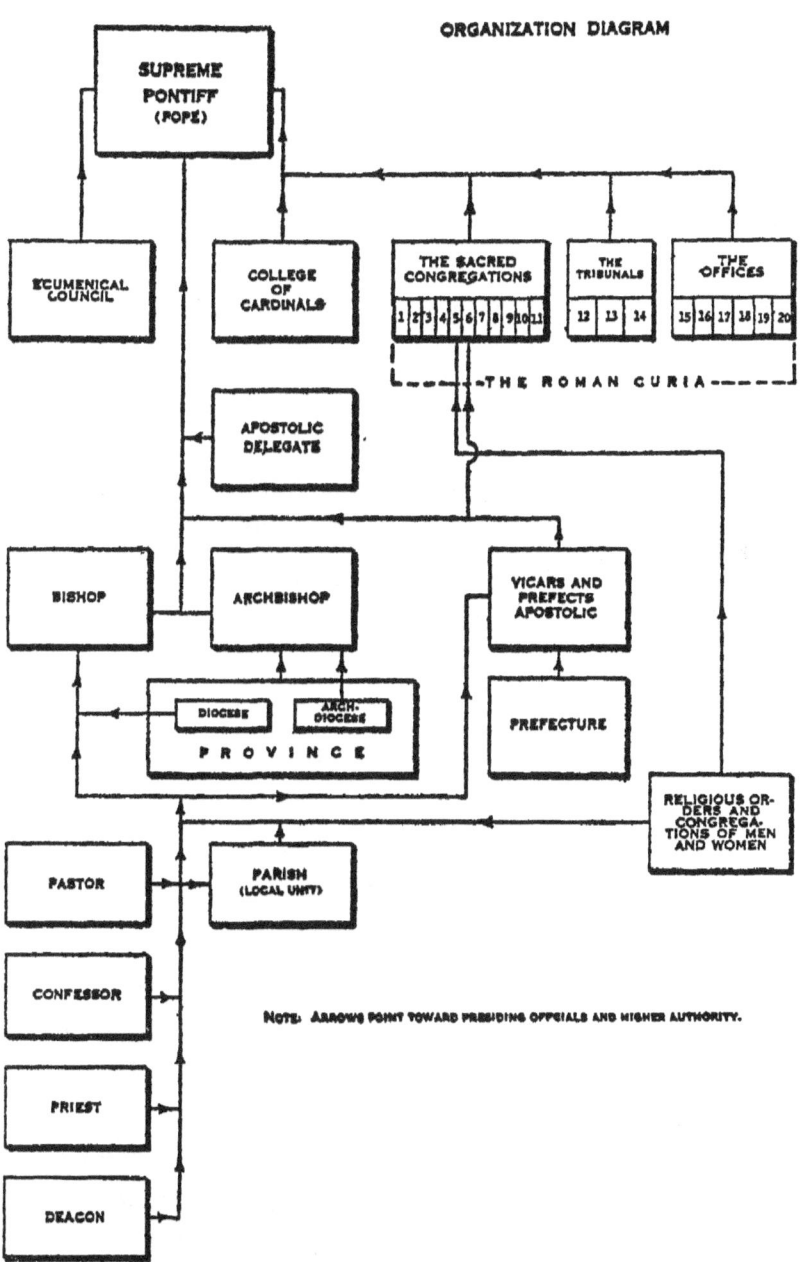

jurisdictional standing, but only their position in the cardinalate. With few exceptions the cardinal priests are archbishops or bishops, and the cardinal deacons are generally priests. In case of the death of the pope the cardinals elect his successor, authority meanwhile being vested in the body of cardinals. Most of the cardinals reside in Rome, and their active duties are chiefly in connection with the various congregations or commissions which have the care of the different departments of church activity.

It is in keeping with the spirit of law in the Roman Church that it pays high honor to the "priestly office." The faithful willingly obey the priest, the priest the bishop, and they all recognize the absolute authority of the Roman Bishop, which is finally settled since the Vatican Council of 1870 and was then formulated as follows:

"That the Roman Pontiff, when he speaks ex cathedra, that is, when, in discharge of the office of pastor and doctor of all Christians by virtue of his supreme Apostolic authority, he defines a doctrine, regarding faith or morals to be held by the Universal Church, by the divine assistance promised to him in blessed Peter, is possessed of that infallibility with which the divine Redeemer willed that his Church should be endowed for defining doctrine regarding faith or morals; and that therefore such definitions of the Roman Pontiff are irreformable of themselves, and not from the consent of the Church."

In consequence of the uniform organization of its statutes, the Roman Church cannot suffer national churches to become independent within the body of the Church. It also can only endure within very narrow limits any individual digressions from ordinary average piety. On this account it has been subject to more partitions than any other church. On the other hand it can comprehend a reunion of scattered Christendom only in a legal submission to the Roman bishop, and therefore officially refuses to join a church union whose members in brotherly love have agreed to recognize the varying peculiarities of the other Christian communions.

Catholic bishops are responsible guardians of the deposit of faith. They are the successors of the Apostles, endowed with their authority and power to teach and govern the Church. Taken singly, they do not inherit the personal endowments of the Apostles; they have neither the gift of inspiration nor of miracles, nor of personal infallibility, nor of universal jurisdiction. They receive no new revelations, no repetitions of old ones; and yet they are infallible in the sense that they cannot collectively be guilty of false teaching, and so lead the whole Church astray. It is possible for individual bishops to desert their duty and fall into heresy, as some have done in times past; but such are quickly cut off from the Church, and lose their position in the teaching body. For a bishop can retain his office only by remaining in communion with his fellow bishops and with the pope; separated from this communion, he ceases to be a member of the teaching Church. It is in this collective body of bishops in communion with each other and with the pope, that the teaching Church properly consists. Consequently it is believed that any doctrine unanimously taught by this collective body, as part of the deposit of faith, must be infallibly correct.

The pope, besides holding the position of bishop over the local Church of Rome, enjoys the twofold prerogative of supreme ruler and of supreme teacher of the whole Church. These prerogatives are believed to have been bestowed on St. Peter by Christ, and to have been inherited by his successors in the See of Rome. As supreme ruler, the pope has power to make disciplinary laws binding on the whole Church. As supreme teacher, he possesses authority to settle disputed points of faith and morals.

When, acting in his highest official capacity of teacher of the Universal Church, the pope defines a point of faith or morals with the intent of binding the whole Church—then it is believed that the decision will be infallible.

In the United States, there is an apostolic delegate, fifteen archbishops, of whom four are cardinals, ninety-nine bishops and approximately 30,000 priests. The special province of the apostolic delegate is the settling of difficulties that may arise in the conduct of the dioceses. An archbishop has the care of his archdiocese. Within each diocese, authority is vested in the bishop, although appeal may be made to the apostolic delegate, and, in the last resort, to one of the congregations in Rome.

In the parish, the pastor is in charge, subject to the bishop; he alone has authority to administer the sacraments, though he has the assistance of other priests as may be needed.

Appointment to a bishopric rests with the Holy See at Rome, but names are recommended by the hierarchy in this country.

The clergy are all those who are tonsured (crown of head shaved-corona). The orders of the clergy consist of those in minor orders, and of subdeacons, deacons, and priests.

There are two recognized divinity schools—preparatory seminary and the grand seminary. On taking the vows of chastity and celibacy, a seminarian is ordained by the bishop as subdeacon, then deacon, then priest. The priest has the privilege of conducting the church services, administering the sacraments, and alone is authorized to celebrate the Mass. The bishops and archbishops and higher orders of the clergy are chosen from the ranks of the priesthood.

There are two important kinds of religious orders—the monastic orders, the members of which take solemn vows of obedience, poverty, and chastity; and the religious congregations of priests and various brotherhoods and sisterhoods. Most of the members of these latter congregations take simple, not perpetual vows.

Ordination is absolutely in the hands of the bishop. The orders also have lay members who take the vows but who are not inducted into the priesthood.

A prominent feature in the organization of the Roman Catholic Church, and an important factor in its history, is the system of ecclesiastical councils. These are general or ecumenical, plenary or national, and provincial. A general council is convoked by the pope, or with his consent, is presided over by him or his legates, and includes all the Catholic bishops of the world. A plenary or national council is an assembly of all the bishops of a country, such as the United States.

The acts of a general council, to be binding, must be confirmed by the pope; those of a plenary or provincial council must be submitted to the Holy See before promulgation, for confirmation, and for any needed correction. The scope of the general council includes doctrine and matters of discipline concerning the church in the whole world.

The procedure and working of these councils are similar to those of an ordinary legislative body. The laity have no voice in the conduct of the church, nor in the choice of the local priest.

The income of the church is from pew rents, plate collections, and offerings for baptisms, marriage ceremonies, masses, etc.

The churches are kept open through the day for individual worship and confession. The liturgy is the same for all Roman Catholic churches, and is in Latin. The sermons and instructions, however, are always in the language spoken by the congregation, and the Scriptures are read in the same language.

The Code of Canon Law. The body of ecclesiastical legislation which had been growing from Apostolic times, had not been codified for a long time, and in consequence was somewhat confused at the beginning of the twentieth century.

In 1904 at the order of Pope Piux X, the work of codifying the laws of the Catholic Church was begun.

A commission of cardinals was appointed for the work, the Supreme Pontiff himself serving as president, and Cardinal Gasparri being appointed secretary. All archbishops were asked to confer with their suffragans and to send word to the commission as to laws which in their judgment needed amendment. Every bishop had a right to keep a representative at Rome to assist at the meetings. The commission divided itself into two committees, one sitting on Sunday, the other on Thursday. Every canon of the code was discussed from 5 to 12 times. A tentative draft was then submitted to the consultors of the Commission and also to all bishops and to those superiors of religious orders who are entitled to attend a General Council. The replies were collected by Cardinal Gasparri, and the Commission once more deliberated upon them. After thirteen years of this kind of work, the code was finished.

The new code was promulgated on the 27th of May (Pentecost) 1917, to be effective the 19th of May (Pentecost) 1918.

The Local Church

Consists of the following:

The Local church is called a parish. Each parish has a church building, and in some cases it may be a cathedral. There may also be a school in connection with the parish. A parish may also have one or more mission churches (churches without a resident pastor).

The size of the parish in area is arbitrarily determined

by the bishop of the diocese who has full authority over the parish and appoints and dismisses the pastor.

Each parish has a pastor (priest) who may have an assistant (also a priest).

Diocese

It is an arbitrary geographic area presided over by a bishop who is the highest authority in the diocese.

Each diocese has four or more diocesan consultors (priests) who are consulted by the bishop on certain matters. In the event of the death of a bishop the consultors elect a priest of the diocese to act until a bishop is appointed by the pope. Names of eligible candidates are usually submitted by the apostolic delegate and usually one from that list is chosen by the pope. The priest who is elected to act until a bishop is appointed does not have power to ordain or confirm.

Each diocese has a diocesan court which consists of a certain number of priests appointed by the bishop. It usually deals with cases concerning matrimony and separation.

A Diocesan Synod is held once every ten years and is called and presided over by the bishop for the discussion of matters generally pertaining to the diocese.

Archdiocese (Metropolitan See)

The archdiocese is the main or principal diocese of a province. It is an arbitrary geographic area presided over by an archbishop who acts in relation to the other bishops of the province as an appeal in matrimonial matters and from him there is an appeal to the Roman Curia.

The archbishop has no jurisdiction directly over the other bishops of the province but may report to the Roman Curia about any bishop who is not acting properly.

Prefecture

A prefecture is an arbitrary geographic area applied to missionary districts which are not developed sufficiently to be a diocese. They are usually presided over by a priest who has all the jurisdiction of a bishop but without the episcopal power of Orders.

Vicariate

A vicariate is the same as a prefecture only more developed and is usually presided over by a bishop. It is subdivided into parishes and quasi-parishes.

Province

A province is an arbitrary geographic area including many dioceses and is presided over by an archbishop with very limited jurisdiction over the other bishops of the province.

Each province has a Provincial Council which is held every twenty years and is presided over by the archbishop and attended by all the bishops of the province. The Council considers problems of the church and determines uniform methods to meet the needs. Its acts are subject to the approval of the Roman Curia.

Priests and Lower Clerics

They are without jurisdiction either in external government or in the forum of the confessional. They belong, however, to a certain diocese and are subject to a certain bishop. This judicial relation is called "incardination." (Canon 111.) A deacon may also baptize and distribute holy communion with the permission of the pastor.

Confessor

He is an ordained priest who has received delegation from the bishop, jurisdiction in the sacramental form, i.e., to exercise in sacramental confession the power (which they receive in their ordination) to forgive sins in the name and by the authority of Jesus Christ. (Canon 874).

Pastor

He is an ordained priest who has been appointed by the bishop of the diocese from among the priests of the diocese to take spiritual care of a limited territory in the diocese, called a parish. All pastors have by law ordinary jurisdiction in what is called the sacramental forum, i.e., for the forgiving of sins in confession. Pastors have besides, in virtue of their office, a certain defined jurisdiction in the government of their parish. (Canon 451; 873.)

Religious Orders and Congregations of Men and Women

It consists of an aggregate of different and varied organizations. All have in common, besides an essential nature, a two-fold dependence, first on the Supreme Pontiff, through the Sacred Congregation of Religious, and secondly, on the bishop, archbishop, or vicar or prefect apostolic (hereafter called the Ordinary of the place) of the place where they are. This dependence varies with the different types of religious societies.

A religious society or institute is an organization approved by ecclesiastical authority, whose members live a common life professing the evangelical counsels (poverty, chastity, obedience).

Orders and Congregations. The vows by which the counsels are professed are of two grades, solemn and simple. Solemn vows are the more irrevocable in the eyes of the church. Religious institutes whose members take solemn vows are called religious Orders; those whose members take only simple vows are called religious Congregations. Both religious Orders and Congregations may be composed entirely of men or entirely of women. Orders and Congregations of men may be composed either of clerics (priests) or laymen, or both.

Pontifical or Diocesan Organization. Every religious Order or Congregation is governed by the general law of the church (the Code of Canon Law) and also by an organic law of its own which is called its Constitution. The Constitutions of all religious Orders must be approved by the Holy See (through the Sacred Congregation of Religious, a unit of the Roman Curia, No. 5 in the diagram).

Exemption. Although the Ordinaries of places (bishops, archbishops, etc.) are endowed with general ecclesiastical jurisdiction for their respective territories, subject to the general laws of the church, yet, according to a very ancient tradition and discipline which is now recognized by the Code of Canon Law, members of religious Orders (as distinguished from religious Congregations) are exempt from the jurisdiction of the Ordinaries of places, except in certain specified matters. The dependence of religious Orders upon the Ordinary of the place is therefore relatively slight.

Vicars and Prefects Apostolic

Vicars apostolic and prefects apostolic govern defined territories in mission countries in the name of the Supreme Pontiff. (Canon 293.) They do not form, as bishops do, an essential part in the constitution of the Church; but they receive a similar jurisdiction. Their territories, which are less perfectly organized than dioceses, are called vicariates or prefectures apostolic, and are divided into smaller divisions called quasi-parishes.

Archbishop

Archbishops, also called metropolitans, are simply bishops of special rank, having their own territory or archdiocese, and having besides a very limited supervisory and provisional authority over certain other independently governed dioceses, which are called Suffragan Sees. (Canon 274.)

Bishop

Bishops holding their jurisdiction directly from the Supreme Pontiff in virtue of their canonical mission, are in charge of the government of the church in particular territories, under the authority of the Roman Pontiff. According to Catholic doctrine, bishops are of divine institution in this sense, that in constituting His Church on earth, Jesus Christ ordained that there should be such officers forming an essential part of the government of His church. The jurisdiction of each individual bishop, however, comes directly and solely from the Supreme Pontiff, and is to be exercised subject to his supreme authority. (Canon 329.)

Apostolic Delegate

Apostolic delegates are personal representatives of the Supreme Pontiff in various parts of the world, either with or without ecclesiastical jurisdiction. (Canon 265.) Some of them have the title of apostolic delegates; their duty is to watch over the state of the Church in the country to which they are sent, and report to the Supreme Pontiff thereon. (Canon 267, No. 2.)

The College of Cardinals

This is called "the Senate of the Roman Pontiff," "his principal counselors and assistants in the government of the Church." (Canon 230.) Individual cardinals are appointed by the pope. The cardinals render service in the government of the Church chiefly through the Roman Curia, the various departments of which, with the exception of the Rota, are made up of membership of cardinals appointed by the pope. Individual cardinals may also be appointed and consecrated bishops of particular sees. In case of vacancy of the Apostolic See, the College of Cardinals has duties and powers which are accurately defined by law, and the chief of which is the election of the new pope. (Canon 241; 160.)

Ecumenical Council

"There can be no Ecumenical Council which is not convoked by the Roman Pontiff. It is the part of the same Roman Pontiff to preside at the Ecumenical Council either in person or through representatives, to determine and designate the matters to be treated and the order to be observed therein, also to transfer, suspend, or dissolve the Council, and to confirm its decrees." (Canon 222.)

The Roman Curia

The Roman Curia represents the departmental organization of the central ecclesiastical government. The power they exercise is that of the pope, and is partly ordinary (i.e., annexed by law to the office in question) and partly delegated. The division between legislative, executive and judicial functions is not perfectly observed; although it may be said in general that the Sacred Congregations are engaged primarily in administration, the tribunals in deciding cases, and the offices in transacting official business. It will be seen that the Sacred Congregations sometimes act as tribunals and exercise a judicial power. They have also a secondary legislative power in the sense that they enact and promulgate administrative rules affecting the application of the general laws of the Church. The Code Commission (No. 20 in the diagram) issues, in response to questions put to it by bishops, authentic interpretations of the law. A bare outline of the principal function of these various units is given below.

The Sacred Congregations

(Numbers correspond to those on chart, page 211)

1. The Holy Office is the first in dignity of the Roman Congregations. It acts both as a tribunal and as an administrative department in regard to matters affecting faith and morals. (Canon 247.)

2. The Sacred Consistorial Congregation is charged with the territorial division of dioceses, and the appointment and general supervision of bishops except in mission countries. (Canon 248.)

3. The Sacred Congregation of the Sacraments has charge of the general discipline regarding the sacraments, and also exercises judicial jurisdiction in certain marriage cases and cases affecting Holy Orders. (Canon 249.)

4. The Sacred Congregation of the Council has charge of the general discipline of the secular clergy and of the laity. (Canon 250.)

5. The Sacred Congregation of Religious: general authority over all religious orders and congregations of men or women. (Canon 251.)

6. The Sacred Congregation of Propaganda: administration of mission countries. (Canon 252.)

7. The Sacred Congregation of Rites: all matters pertaining to sacred rites and ceremonies. (Canon 253.) It acts as a special tribunal in the canonization of Saints. (Canon 1999.)

8. The Sacred Congregation of Ceremonies: cere-

monies of the Papal Chapel, and those in which cardinals take part. (Canon 254.)

9. The Sacred Congregation For Extraordinary Ecclesiastical Affairs: appointment of bishops and other matters which require negotiation with civil governments (e.g., where Concordats are in effect). (Canon 255.)

10. The Sacred Congregation of Seminaries and Universities: regulation of studies and administration of seminaries and universities founded by ecclesiastical authority. (Canon 256.)

11. The Sacred Congregation for the Oriental Church: general authority over those Oriental Churches which are in union with Rome. (Canon 257.)

The Tribunals

12. The Sacred Penitentiary: a tribunal for the form of conscience; has a sub-commission for Indulgences. (Canon 258.)

13. The Sacred Roman Rota: a tribunal having appellate jurisdiction in marriage and other cases. (Canon 259; 1598.)

14. The Supreme Tribunal of the Signatura: the supreme ordinary appellate tribunal under the Supreme Pontiff. (Canon 259; 1602.)

The Offices

15. The Apostolic Chancery: expedition of the more important Papal Letters and Bulls. (Canon 260.)

16. The Apostolic Datary: investigation of candidates

for certain benefices; and other administrative details regarding benefices. (Canon 261.)

17. The Apostolic Camera: administration of the temporal goods of the Holy See, especially during its vacancy. (Canon 262.)

18. The Office of the Papal Secretary of State: dealings with civil governments and other powers defined by law. (Canon 263.)

19. The Secretariates of Briefs to Princes and of Latin Letters; composition of this correspondence at the direction of the Supreme Pontiff. (Canon 264.)

20. The Pontifical Commission For the Authentic Interpretation of the Code of Canon Law. This body deserves a place apart, as it is not strictly an "office" in the same sense as the other offices with which it is classed in the diagram. It is not mentioned in the Code of Canon Law as forming part of the Curia. The Commission was created by a Motu Proprio of Benedict XV, 15 September 1917, after the completion and promulgation of the Code of Canon Law, but before the date when it was to become effective. As its name indicates the function of this Commission is the authentic interpretation of the Canons of the Code. It fulfills this function by delivering from time to time brief replies to definite questions proposed by bishops, touching the interpretation of various canons. Its replies are officially promulgated, as are also the important acts of the other departments of the Roman Curia, in the Acta Apostolicae Sedis, the official commentary of the Vatican. The replies of the Code Commission when duly promulgated have the force of law. (Canon 17.)

The Supreme Pontiff (Pope)

The government of the Catholic Church is essentially monarchial. This point is made clear by the chart which shows the Supreme Pontiff as the head and fount of all jurisdiction. The Code of Canon Law expresses this essential Catholic doctrine in these words:

"The Roman Pontiff, the successor of St. Peter in the primacy, has not merely the primacy of honor but the supreme and full power of jurisdiction in the universal Church, both in things pertaining to faith and morals and in those which concern the discipline and government of the Church over the entire world. This power is truly episcopal, ordinary and immediate, both over all and each of the churches and over all and each of the pastors and faithful, independent of any human authority." (Canon 218.)

CHAPTER XVI

UNITARIANS

Those adhering to the Unitarian doctrines are located principally in the United States and Great Britain. Missionary work is carried on in practically all foreign countries.

Historical Sketch

Unitarianism of today originated, historically, in the first half century of the Protestant Reformation. The word Unitarian is now commonly used to designate those who believe in the unity of the personality of God, as distinct from Trinitarians, who believe in three Divine Persons. The origin of the name is disputed, but it seems to have appeared first in Hungary, in the new Latin form of Unitarius, about 1570. It was first officially used in Transylvania, in 1638, and the English word is now used by the Associations of England and America, though it is not found till 1687. The common names for Unitarians were at first Anti-trinitarians, Arians, Socinians, Racovians, and others. In America, they are often called Unitarian Congregationalists, being the Unitarian branch of the Congregationalist body since the division at the beginning of this century. In England, for a similar reason, they are often called Presbyterians.

In England, Unitarianism gradually developed during

the eighteenth century, largely under Socinian influences, and chiefly among the Presbyterian churches, though there were also important accessions from other religious bodies. While such men as Newton, Locke, Milton, and Penn, in the seventeenth century, are known to have held Unitarian views, no movement toward a distinct denomination began until late in the eighteenth century; the most distinguished leaders of Unitarianism, since its separate organization, have been Joseph Priestly, Theophilus Lindsey, and James Martineau.

More Unitarians came from the Presbyterians than from any other body, nearly half of the churches of this faith now existing in England having been once Presbyterian, many of them still retaining that name. The founder of the present organized body of English Unitarians was the Reverend Theophilus Lindsey, who left the Church of England and gathered a Unitarian congregation in Essex Street, London, in 1774.

In America, Unitarianism developed out of New England Congregationalism, whose churches had as a rule unwittingly left the way open for doctrinal changes, by requiring members upon joining the church simply to join in a covenant, rather than to subscribe to a creed. Thus, many of the Congregational churches of eastern Massachusetts, including most of the oldest and most important ones, gradually moved far toward Unitarian beliefs in the second half of the eighteenth century, though the first church distinctly to avow such beliefs was the Episcopal King's Chapel at Boston in 1785. These churches preferred to call themselves simply Liberal

Christians, and the name Unitarian was only slowly and reluctantly accepted.

The formation of a new denomination out of the liberal wing of the Congregational Church was a gradual process, which went on in one congregation after another. The cleavage was hastened by the election of Henry Ware, a liberal, in spite of orthodox protests, as professor of theology at Harvard University in 1805. The conservatives in 1815, fastened the name "Unitarian" upon the liberals, and gradually refused them fellowship, desiring in this way to exclude them from the denomination. At length, in 1819, William Ellery Channing of Boston, acknowledged leader of the liberals, preached an ordination sermon at Baltimore which defined and defended the views held by Unitarians and which was thenceforth accepted by them as their platform.

In 1825, the American Unitarian Association was formed to do aggressive missionary work and to promote the interests of the churches concerned; thus the new denomination became separately organized. The Unitarians of this period were much averse to fostering sectarian spirit. They had been only loosely welded together, and their own fundamental principles were not clearly settled, so that for nearly 40 years the denomination was stagnant and was divided and weakened by internal controversy centering mainly about the question of miracles. By the end of the Civil War this controversy had been largely outgrown; a national conference was organized in 1865, and a period of rapid extension and aggressive denominational life ensued, which has continued to the present time. For a generation past, emphasis has been laid much less upon doctrinal points than upon personal religion, moral advancement, and civic and social reform.

Doctrine

Unitarians have no creed or official theology. They merely have "statements" of faith. The most popular being: "The Fatherhood of God; the Brotherhood of man; the Leadership of Jesus; salvation by character; the progress of mankind, onward and upward forever."

But this is in no sense final or authoritative, it is simply an attempt to set forth the things most commonly believed. There are forms for admission into Unitarian church-membership, but in no case is any sort of doctrinal test imposed or implied. This arises not from any lack of religious belief or conviction among Unitarians, but, first, because they hold that belief in and frequent recital of a creed does not necessarily make a person Christian or even religious; secondly, Unitarians feel very strongly that no church or council ought or has any right to require any person to commit himself for all time to some particular form of worship, or to sacraments or dogmas, no matter how true they may seem to be.

Believing in the spiritual imperfection of all persons and institutions, past as well as present Unitarians feel that changeless creeds and sacraments make it impossible or unnecessarily difficult to press forward to a finer spiritual quality in life. For this reason, Unitarians refuse

UNITARIANS

to have anything to do with finalities and infallibilities in religion.

There is nevertheless a Unitarian faith which binds Unitarians together in a common purpose and a sort of common understanding of religious matters. It has been expressed thus: "Just as an association of scientists is constituted and sustained, not by the adoption of a theory, however certain, but by a common purpose or aim, so a church is possible, by virtue of the common purpose to seek contact with the divine life and to find mutual expression of the experience."

Although Unitarians are free to formulate each his own conclusion, there runs through all the consequent diversity of opinion, strands of a common faith; on all great religious issues, there is among them quite a strong agreement.

"Every race has its Bible, and all Scripture is given by inspiration. But while we gladly recognize the merits and oft-time beauty of other sacred writings—such as the Vedas, Zendavesta, Shu Kings and Koran—we yet hold that, for us at least, the Jewish and Christian Scriptures are superior to them in literary, moral and religious values, because they flowed out of a higher conception of God and man, and human and social duty." Thus is summarized the Unitarian belief in the Bible.

Unitarianism may be defined in the most general terms as the religious doctrine of those holding belief in one God in one person (as distinguished from the Trinitarian belief in one God in three persons) and the related belief in the strict humanity of Jesus Christ (as contrasted with the belief in His Deity). While Unitarians assert that these beliefs were held in the first Christian centuries before ever the Trinitarian dogmas were developed, yet the Unitarianism of today originated historically in the first half century of the Protestant Reformation.

The constitution of the General Conference states simply that "These churches accept the religion of Jesus, holding in accordance with His teaching that practical religion is summed up in love to God and love to man." The declared object of the American Unitarian Association is "to diffuse the knowledge and promote the interests of pure Christianity." The covenant most generally used in local churches reads: "In the love of truth and in the spirit of Jesus, we unite for the worship of God and the service of man."

The most distinguishing marks of Unitarianism today are its insistence upon absolute freedom in belief, its reliance upon the supreme guidance of reason, its tolerance of difference in religious opinion, its devotion to education and philanthropy, and its emphasis upon character, as the principles of fundamental importance in religion. There is, however, a general consensus upon the unipersonality of God, the strict humanity of Jesus, the essential dignity and perfectibility of human nature, the natural character of the Bible, and the hope for the ultimate salvation of all souls, which is somewhat different from the views traditionally taught on these points.

Organization and Government

The government of the Unitarian Church is congregational in form, each congregation being entirely inde-

UNITARIANS 235

THE UNITARIAN CHURCH
ORGANIZATION DIAGRAM

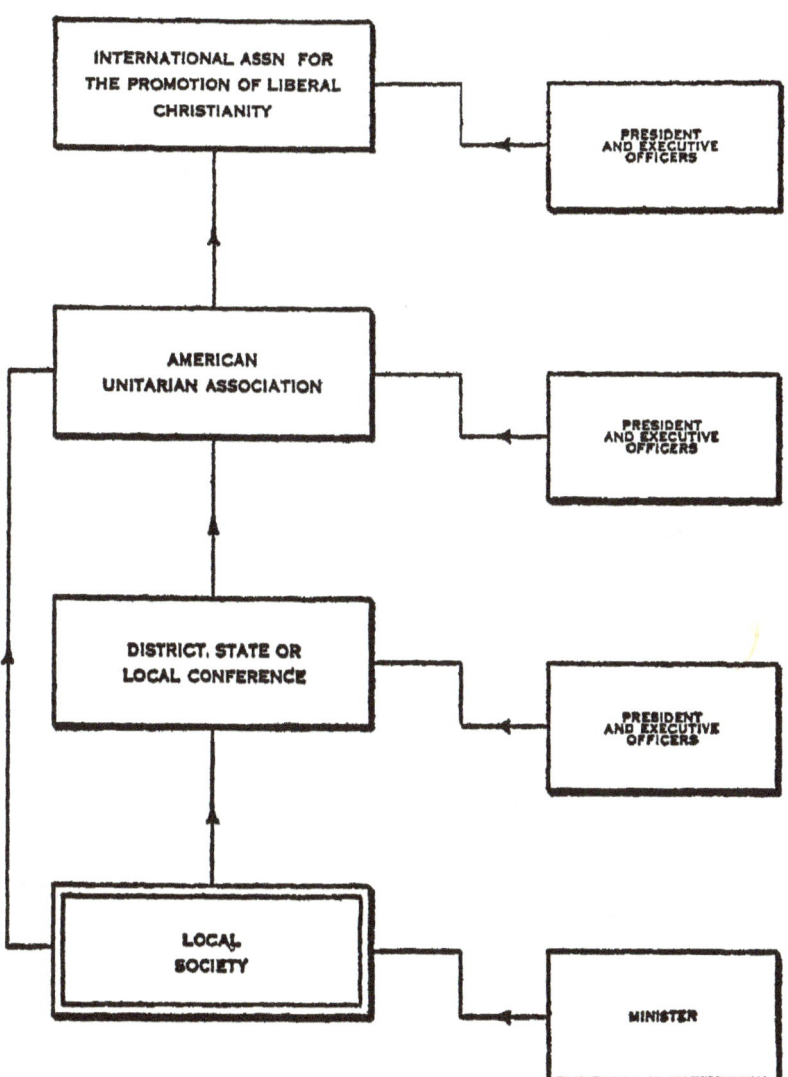

NOTE: ARROWS POINT TOWARD LARGER ADVISORY BODIES, WHOSE PRINCIPAL FUNCTION IS THE PROMOTION OF UNITARIAN IDEALS IN GREATER AREAS. ALL BODIES OR ASSOCIATIONS ABOVE THAT OF THE LOCAL SOCIETY (CHURCH) ARE FOR ADVISORY PURPOSES ONLY AS THEY HAVE NO JURISDICTION IN MATTERS OF DOCTRINE OR GOVERNMENT. EXCEPTION IS MADE WHERE A LOCAL SOCIETY RECEIVES FINANCIAL AID FROM THE AMERICAN UNITARIAN ASSOCIATION. OVER SUCH AIDED SOCIETIES (CHURCHES) THE AMERICAN UNITARIAN ASSOCIATION EXERCISES A LIMITED JURISDICTION.

THE DOUBLE LINE AROUND THE LOCAL CHURCH INDICATES ITS INDEPENDENT OR AUTONOMOUS CHARACTER.

pendent of all the others. But for purposes of fellowship, mutual counsel, and the promotion of common ends, they unite in local or state conferences, in a General Conference (American Unitarian Association) meeting biennially, and in an international congress formed "to open communication with those in all lands who are striving to unite pure religion and perfect liberty and to increase fellowship and cooperation among them."

They regard the church as "the voluntary association of those who find fellowship in the religion of the spirit. It is not the source from which religion is to be drawn, rather is it a product of religion; an organization for comradeship in the growing life of the spirit."

Besides the national missionary organization, the American Unitarian Association, with headquarters at Boston, and offices at New York, Chicago, and San Francisco, other national organizations include the Alliance of Unitarian Women, the Unitarian Sunday School Society, the Young People's Religious Union, the Laymen's League, the Unitarian Temperance Society, etc.

The Local Church or Society

Consists of the following:

>Minister
>Board of Trustees
>President
>Vice-President
>Secretary
>Treasurer

UNITARIANS

Women's Alliance
Laymen's League
Young People's Society
School of Religious Education
Junior Alliances

Each local society (congregation) is supreme in all matters of doctrine and government. All higher bodies, and organizations and their officers, are for advisory and administrative purposes only (administrative only when a financial interest in local society or church is involved).

Each local society that makes its annual contribution to the American Unitarian Association is permitted to send two delegates to the American Unitarian Association Convention.

District, State or Local Conference

It consists of an unlimited membership from the local societies (churches). It has a president, board of directors, secretary and treasurer. It generally meets yearly.

Its main purpose is to act as an advisory conference and to promote fellowship among the societies within its area. It has, however, no jurisdiction in doctrine or government, over any local society.

American Unitarian Association (General Conference)

The American Unitarian Association has a board of directors, president, vice-presidents, secretary and treasurer.

Due to the merger of the General Conference with the American Unitarian Association, the Association holds a meeting, as the "General Conference," every second year and preferably outside of New England. The Association meets annually in Massachusetts due to its incorporation in that state.

Delegates to its sessions are arranged on the following basis: "Each member church shall be entitled to be represented at all meetings of the Association by its minister or ministers and two accredited lay delegates for the first fifty voting members or fractional part thereof and by one additional delegate for each additional fifty voting members, chosen during the year at any regular or special meeting; all other member societies shall be represented by the President and two other accredited delegates, only, chosen as aforesaid."

This organization with its divisions acts in an advisory and administrative capacity. It has, however, no jurisdiction in doctrine or government, over any local society or church.

It has associated organizations such as General Alliance of Unitarian and other Liberal Christian Women, Laymen's League, Unitarian Ministerial Union and Young People's Religious Union, together with various executive departments.

International Association for the Promotion of Liberal Christianity and Religious Freedom

This consists of an unlimited membership from any or all Unitarian Societies throughout the world. It has no administrative function but merely acts for fellowship and the promotion of Unitarian ideals throughout the world. It meets once every two years in Holland.

ACKNOWLEDGMENT

On the following pages is a list of those of each denominational group who cooperated in the compilation of the chart, either supplying the material, making suggestions, or checking and confirming the answers as applicable to their respective denominational group or column of the chart.

Because of the necessity of brevity in the condensation of the material, the wording and contents of each answer were carefully checked for the purpose of having the answers as authentic as possible.

Where the church body had not set out its statement of belief in a condensed form, the individual and personal beliefs, in so far as they were understood to be generally accepted, were considered.

In each denomination there are the modernists, fundamentalists, liberalists and conservatists, all of which were considered. However, the various representatives confined their material only to the generally accepted doctrinal interpretations.

Other important Christian denominations could have been included in the summary chart; however, on close analysis, many are seen to closely parallel, in doctrine and church government, those here considered.

Authorities Who Contributed the Material Appearing on the Comparative Chart

ADVENTISTS

Rev. E. Kotz, D. D.,
Associate Secretary, General Conference of Seventh-day Adventists, Washington, D. C.

Rev. B. W. Brown, D. D.,
First Seventh-day Adventist Church, Lodi, California.

BAPTISTS

Rev. James S. West, D. D.,
First Baptist Church, San Francisco, California.

Rev. W. Richard Sloman, D. D.,
Baptist Church, Rochester, New York.

Rev. Brewster Adams, D. D.,
First Baptist Church, Reno, Nevada.

EPISCOPAL

Rt. Rev. Edward L. Parsons, D. D.,
Bishop, The Episcopal Diocese of California, San Francisco, Calif.

Rt. Rev. Arthur W. Moulton, D. D.,
Bishop, The Episcopal Church in Utah, Salt Lake City, Utah.

Very Rev. Bayard H. Jones, D. D.,
Dean, Trinity Cathedral, Reno, Nevada.

ACKNOWLEDGMENT

CHURCH OF JESUS CHRIST OF LATTER-DAY SAINTS *(Mormon)*
  James E. Talmage, LL. D.,
   Of the Council of the Twelve Apostles, Salt Lake City, Utah.
  John A. Widtsoe, Ph. D.,
   Of the Council of the Twelve Apostles, Salt Lake City, Utah.

EASTERN ORTHODOX *(Catholic)*
  Rev. C. H. Demetry, D. D.,
   Greek Orthodox Church Schools of America, Chicago, Illinois.
  Rev. G. Prosor, D. D.,
   Eastern Orthodox Church Society of San Francisco, California.

LUTHERANS
  Rev. Ralph H. Long, D. D.,
   Executive Director, National Lutheran Council, New York City, New York.
  Rev. F. E. Martens, D. D.,
   Missouri Synod, Martinez, California.
  Rev. F. E. Schumann, D. D.,
   St. John's Evangelical Lutheran Church, Salt Lake City, Utah.

METHODISTS
  Rev. Ray S. Dum, D. D.,
   Central Methodist Episcopal Church, Spokane, Washington.

Rev. Alfred J. Case, D. D.,
  Wesley Methodist Church, Richmond, California.
Rev. W. T. Scott, D. D.,
  Cameron Methodist Episcopal Church, Denver, Colorado.

PRESBYTERIAN
  Rev. Jesse H. Baird, D. D.,
    Pres. Presbyterian Theological Seminary, San Anselmo, California.
  M. K. W. Heicher, D. D.,
          and
  J. E. Wishart, D. D.,
    San Francisco Theological Seminary, San Francisco, California.
  Rev. Wm. Moll Case, D. D.,
    Federated Presbyterian-Congregational Church, Reno, Nevada.

ROMAN CATHOLIC
  Duane G. Hunt, Bishop,
    Salt Lake Diocese, Salt Lake City, Utah.
  Rev. Francis X. Busch, S. J.,
    Professor of Dogmatic Theology at St. Mary of the Lake Seminary, Mundelein, Illinois.

UNITARIAN
  Raymond C. Bragg, D. D.,
    Secretary Western Unitarian Conference, Chicago, Illinois.
  Rev. Jacob Trapp, D. D.,
    First Unitarian Society, Salt Lake City, Utah.

ACKNOWLEDGMENT

Contributing Authorities Who Helped in Working out the Church Organization Diagrams

ADVENTISTS, SEVENTH DAY
Rev. E. Kotz, D. D.,
Associate Secretary, General Conference of Seventh-day Adventists, Washington, D. C.

BAPTISTS
Rev. William A. Hill, D. D.,
Secretary of Missionary Education, Northern Baptist Convention, New York City, New York.

CATHOLIC, ROMAN
Duane G. Hunt, Bishop,
Salt Lake Diocese, Salt Lake City, Utah.
Rev. Francis X. Busch, S. J.,
St. Mary of the Lake Seminary, Mundelein, Illinois.

CATHOLIC, EASTERN ORTHODOX
Rev. Athenagoras Cavadas, D. D.,
Greek Archdiocese of North and South America, Long Island, New York.

CONGREGATIONAL AND CHRISTIAN CHURCHES
Rev. Herbert W. Gates, D. D.,
General Secretary, Congregational Education Society, Boston, Mass.

Rev. Charles C. Burton, D. D.,
  Secretary, General Council of Congregational and Christian Churches, New York City, New York.

Disciples of Christ
Rev. H. O. Pritchard, D. D.,
  General Secretary, Board of Education of Disciples of Christ, Indianapolis, Indiana.

Episcopal, Protestant
Rt. Rev. Arthur W. Moulton,
  Bishop of Utah, Salt Lake City, Utah.
Very Rev. Bayard H. Jones,
  Dean of Trinity Cathedral, Reno, Nevada.

Church of Jesus Christ of Latter-Day Saints
John A. Widtsoe, Ph. D.,
  Of the Council of the Twelve Apostles, Salt Lake City, Utah.
James E. Talmage, LL. D.,
  Of the Council of the Twelve Apostles, Salt Lake City, Utah.

Lutheran
Rev. A. C. Keck, D. D.,
  Nevada Conference, Missouri Synod, Reno, Nevada.
Rev. F. E. Schumann, D. D.,
  St. Johns Evangelical Lutheran Church, Salt Lake City, Utah.

ACKNOWLEDGMENT

METHODISTS
Rev. Miron A. Morrill, D. D.,
  Director, Board of Education, Methodist Episcopal Church, Chicago, Illinois.
Rev. Rollin H. Ayres, D. D.,
  First Methodist Episcopal Church, Salt Lake City, Utah.

PRESBYTERIAN
Rev. Harold McA. Robinson, D. D.,
  Secretary Board of Christian Education of the Presbyterian Church in U. S. A., Philadelphia, Pa.
Dr. H. W. Reherd, D. D.,
  President Westminster College, Salt Lake City, Utah.

CHURCH OF CHRIST, SCIENTISTS
Lucia C. Warren,
  Secretary, The Christian Science Board of Directors, Boston, Mass.
Clarence I. Waters,
  Committee on Publication, State of Utah, Salt Lake City, Utah.

UNITARIAN
Rev. Walter R. Hunt, D. D.,
  Secretary, American Unitarian Association, Boston, Mass.
Rev. Jacob Trapp, D. D.,
  First Unitarian Society, Salt Lake City, Utah.

SPECIAL REFERENCES

The Year Book of the Churches and The Handbook of the Churches published for The Federal Council of the Churches of Christ in America.*

The Schaff-Herzog Encyclopedia of Religious Knowledge, 12 volumes.

The Churches of the Federal Council—edited by Charles S. Macfarland.

Creeds of Christendom, 3 volumes—by Philip Schaff. These contain the full text in their original language, with complete translations into English, the Ecumenical Creeds and the creeds of the following churches: Greek Church, Roman Church, Evangelical Protestant Churches, Evangelical Lutheran Church, Evangelical Reformed Churches and Modern Protestant creeds.

Religious Bodies, 2 volumes—compiled by the United States Bureau of Census.

Encyclopedia of Religion and Ethics, 12 volumes—by James Hastings.

The Catholic Encyclopedia, 15 volumes.

---

*The Federal Council of Churches of Christ in America is an official and ecclesiastically organized body to which representatives are sent by all churches comprising this organization.

The Federal Council itself has no authority over the constituent bodies adhering to it; nor to draw up a common creed or form of government or of worship or in any way to limit the full autonomy of the Christian bodies adhering to it, but is limited to the expression of its counsel and the recommending of a course of action in matters of common interest to the churches. In this capacity it represents 28 different Christian denominations.

SPECIAL REFERENCES

The Seven Ecumenical Councils—by Henry R. Percival.

The World's Parliament of Religions—by John H. Barrows.

Ecumenical Handbook of the Churches of Christ—by D. C. Fairbanks, Germany.

APPENDIX

Christian Religions in the United States—*Continued*

Group	Denomination	Number of Bodies	Rank as to Membership	Approx. date of first organization in America
I. Reformed				
	Adventists	5	20	1845
	Am. Rescue Workers	1	47	1884
	Apostolic Overcoming Holy Church	1	54	1916
	Assemblies of God	1	23	1914
	Baptists	18	2	1639
	Brethren (Dunkers)	5	21	1729
	Brethren (Plymouth)	6	41	1855
	Brethren (River)	3	52	1770
	Christian and Missionary Alliance	1	36	1887
	Christian Union	1	46	1864
	Church of Christ (Holiness), U.S.A.	1	51	1894
	Church of God (Anderson, Indiana)	5	29	1880
	Church of God General Assembly	1	43	1888
	Church of God in Christ	1	19	1859
	Churches of the Living God	2	44	1889
	Church of the Nazarene	1	24	1907
	Churches of Christ	2	12	1810
	Churches of God in N. A. (Gen'l. Elder.)	1	37	1830
	Congregational and Christian Churches	1	9	1620
	Disciples of Christ	1	7	1810
	Evangelical Churches	2	15	1803
	Evangelical & Reformed Church	1	10	1934
	Evangelistic Associations	10	39	1886
	Federated Churches	1	30	1887
	Free Christian Zion	1	64	1905
	Friends (Quakers)	4	27	1724
	Holiness Churches	3	61	1896
	Independent Congregations	1	35	1780
	Int. Church Four-Square Gospel	1	16	1923
	Lutherans	19	4	1648

APPENDIX 249

CHRISTIAN RELIGIONS IN THE UNITED STATES—*Continued*

Group	Denomination	Number of Bodies	Rank as to Membership	Approx. date of first organization in America
I. Reformed—*Continued*				
	Mennonites	15	25	1683
	Methodists	19	3	1735
	Moravians	3	34	1734
	New Apostolic Church	1	55	1850
	Original Church of God	1	58	1886
	Pentecostal Churches	2	33	1895
	Pilgrim Holiness Church	1	42	1897
	Presbyterians	9	5	1611
	Protestant Episcopal Church	1	6	1607
	Reformed Churches	4	14	1628
	Reformed Episcopal Church	1	48	1873
	Salvation Army	1	17	1880
	Scandinavian Evangelicals	3	31	1873
	Schwenkfelders	1	59	1734
	Social Brethren	1	60	1867
	United Brethren	3	13	1800
	Volunteers of America	1	38	1896
	TOTAL	168		

CHRISTIAN RELIGIONS IN THE UNITED STATES

Group	Denomination	Number of Bodies	Rank as to Membership	Approx. date of first organization in America
II. Catholics				
	Eastern (Orthodox)	11	8	1792
	Eastern Separate	1	26	1907
	Old Catholic Church (American)	1	40	1927
	Polish National Catholic Church of America	1	22	1904
	Roman (Western)	7	1	1565
	Total	21		
III. Church of Jesus Christ of Latter-day				
	Saints (Mormons)	2	11	1830
IV. Unitarians				
	Christadelphians	1	56	1844
	Unitarians	1	28	1785
	Universalists	1	32	1785
	Total	3		
V. Philosophic				
	Am. Ethical Union	1	57	1876
	Church of Christ, Scientist	2	18	1879
	Gen. Convention of New Jerusalem, U. S. A.	2	49	1792
	Divine Science Church	1	50	1885
	Liberal Church of America	1	63	1914
	Spiritualists	3	45	1848
	Theosophical Societies	3	53	1875
	Temple Society in America	1	65	1863
	Vendanta Society	1	62	1898
	Total	15		

INDEX

Acknowledgment of Authorities, 239
Adventists: historical sketch, 33; doctrine, 34; organization and government, 36; organization diagram, 37
Apostles' Creed, 21
Arminianism, Doctrine of, 28
Athanasian Creed, 23
Augsburg Confession, 27
Authorities contributing material for Comparative Chart, 240

Baptists: historical sketch, 43; doctrine, 50; division of Baptists, 51; Northern Baptist Convention, 52; Southern Baptist Convention, 53; Negro Baptists, 54; organization and government, 55; organization diagram, 56

Christian Religions in the United States, 248
Church of Christ, Scientist: historical sketch, 62; doctrine, 64; organization and government, 66; organization diagram, 67
Church of England (Episcopal): historical sketch, 130; doctrine, 132; organization and government, 141; organization diagram, 142
Church of Jesus Christ of Latter-day Saints: ˙historical sketch, 69; Division: Reorganized Church of Jesus Christ of Latter-day Saints, 71; doctrine, 73; organization and government, 79; organization diagram, 80
Comparative Chart of Doctrinal Questions, *see back cover*
Congregational and Christian Churches: historical sketch, 94; doctrine, 97; organization and government, 99; organization diagram, 100

Disciples of Christ: historical sketch, 106; doctrine, 107; organization and government, 109; organization diagram, 110

Eastern Orthodox Churches: historical sketch, 114; doctrine, 118; divisions, 120; organization and ˙government, 121; organization diagram, 122
Episcopal (*see Church of England*)

Formal Christian Creeds, 20
Forms of Church Government, 16

Lutherans: historical sketch, 152; doctrine, 156; divisions of Lutherans, 158; United Lutheran Churches in America, 158; National Lutheran Council, 159; Synodical Conference of North America, 159; independent congregations, 162; organization and government, 162; organization diagram, 163

Methodists: historical sketch, 170; doctrine, 174; divisions of Methodists, 176; organization and government, 177; organization diagram, 178

Nicene Creed, 22

Presbyterians: historical sketch, 190; doctrine, 195; divisions of Presbyterians, 196; organization and government, 197; organization diagram, 198

Reformation, the, 29

Roman Catholic Church: historical sketch, 203; doctrine, 206; organization and government, 210; organization diagram, 211

Seventh-day Adventists, 34

Special References, 246

Thirty-nine Articles of the Church of England, the, 28

Unitarians: historical sketch, 229; doctrine, 232; organization and government, 234; organization diagram, 235

Westminster Confession, the, 28

www.ingramcontent.com/pod-product-compliance
Lightning Source LLC
Chambersburg PA
CBHW021837220426
43663CB00005B/289